THE ESSENTIAL BOOK OF SU DOKU 2

To generate unique Su Doku puzzles for this book, Pete Sinden developed a dedicated computer program based on techniques from intelligent systems, game theory and logic programming. Any reader wishing to learn more about his **SudokuMania** puzzle generator, or find more puzzles, should visit his website at **www.sudokumania.com.**

Pete Sinden is an internationally accredited expert in artificial intelligence. He holds degrees from Oxford University, the University of Georgia and University College London. He set up and ran his own successful technology business resulting in his computer models being adopted as standard in a hundred American universities. Having sold his company he returned to the UK and worked in a senior position with a leading British charity, where he was instrumental in creating businesses to give opportunities to disadvantaged individuals. Pete now lives in London where he works with academics to harness his technological and business skills to bring new inventions to market.

He is the author of *The Essential Book of Su Doku.*

THE ESSENTIAL BOOK OF SU DOKU 2

	4	9	6		1	3	7	
	6		7		8		1	
	9	8	3	5	4	7	6	
				9				
5								4
	3	7	1		2	6	5	
		6	5	7	9	2		
				6				

PETE SINDEN

ATRIA BOOKS
New York London Toronto Sydney

ATRIA BOOKS
1230 Avenue of the Americas
New York, NY 10020

Published by arrangement with Michael O'Mara Books Limited

Originally published in Great Britain in 2005
by Michael O'Mara Books Limited

ISBN-13: 978-0-7432-9167-5
ISBN-10: 0-7432-9167-0

5 7 9 10 8 6 4

First Atria Books trade paperback edition September 2005

Manufactured in the United States of America

INTRODUCTION

What is Su Doku? And why are we hearing about it, and seeing it everywhere, in newspapers and magazines and, now, books?

Put simply, Su Doku (or "SuDoku," or "Su-doku") is a number-placement puzzle based on a square grid, typically 9 squares by 9, giving 81 squares in all. The puzzle is further divided (by bold gridlines) into 9 boxes or "regions," each a square measuring 3 squares by 3. Figures from 1 to 9 (known as "givens") are already inserted in some of the squares; to complete the puzzle, a player must insert the missing numbers so that each row, each column, and each region contains the numbers 1 to 9 once and once only, without any repeats. The level of difficulty depends upon the number of givens in any puzzle, and the ease with which a player can compute the missing numbers by the use of logic.

Su Doku is thought to have been invented by the great Swiss mathematician Leonhard Euler (1707–83). During the 1980s the game became something of a craze in Japan (hence its Japanese title, apparently from *su*, "number," and *doku*, "single"); in the United States it was published for many years under the title *Number Place*. In Britain late in 2004, the first puzzle appeared in *The Times* newspaper, and the game is now gaining a worldwide following.

Solving Su Doku puzzles demands no mathematical skills, nor does one need an aptitude for crosswords or chess problems. Instead, it requires an ability to think logically, a good deal of patience and a certain steely determination. As readers of this book will find, though, it is also utterly engrossing.

If you liked *The Essential Book of Su Doku*, here is a second volume to keep you entertained!

Puzzle 1

			8				7	9
	8			4	7			
4	7			2	6	3	8	
5		8					6	
9	6						5	2
	4					9		1
	2	3	5	7			4	8
			4	6			1	
6	5				8			

LEVEL 1

Puzzle 2

6		7			8	1		3
					4			9
4		5		3		7		
		1			6	5		4
5	3						9	2
7		9	5			3		
		8		2		9		7
2			9					
9		3	7			2		5

Level 1

Puzzle 3

	2	1	6		3	7	4	
				5		6		
	7		4	1	9	5		
8		6						
	1	9	8		5	2	6	
						1		8
		8	2	6	7		1	
		2		3				
	6	7	1		8	3	2	

Level 1

Puzzle 4

	9		6		8	2		
	6	7			1	5		
				9			6	3
	4	5	9					8
	7		1		4		5	
1					6	3	2	
2	1			6				
		6	5			8	1	
		4	8		2		3	

Level 1

Puzzle 5

	6			9	7	8	3	5
		5		2				1
3				4				
	5	2	6	7	4			
		7	8		2	5		
			9	5	3	7	1	
				6				9
7				8		4		
5	8	9	4	3			7	

Level 1

Puzzle 6

					3	4		
1	9		7	8				3
7		3					1	5
3		4	6		1		7	9
				9				
9	5		4		7	2		8
5	2					7		6
4				7	6		5	1
		7	5					

Level 1

Puzzle 7

	3			4				6
		1			3	7		8
5		4	8			9		
2	1	5						9
3		7				6		5
4						8	1	3
		2			1	5		7
6		3	4			2		
1				7			6	

Level 1

Puzzle 8

				4		5		3
3			1				7	2
5	9		2		6		4	8
				5		7		
		6	3		9	2		
		4		1				
2	6		5		8		1	9
1	7				3			5
4		5		6				

Level 1

Puzzle 9

7							5	8
		8	2	5		1		9
								7
			4	2	6	7		
9	4	7	5		8	6	2	3
		1	7	9	3			
8								
2		6		8	1	4		
5	9							6

Level 1

Puzzle 10

	8			6	7	5		
	5			4	1			
	7		5			6	2	1
	9			8	4			3
			7		2			
1			3	9			8	
2	3	8			5		4	
			4	1			3	
		4	8	2			6	

Level 1

Puzzle 11

			9	6		2	4	
		5		4	1	7		
8		6	3	2	7			
4			5		3			
		9				4		
			4		8			1
			7	3	4	1		5
		4	1	5		9		
	1	2		8	9			

Level 1

Puzzle 12

	3			7		9	8	5
		9	4		5	2	6	7
5								4
				1		8		
	1		6	8	4		9	
		8		5				
7								9
9	5	1	2		7	3		
8	6	4		9			1	

Level 1

Puzzle 13

				2	3	5		8
				4		9		
			8	5		7	3	
7			1		5		9	
8	9	5	3	7	2	6	4	1
	1		6		4			5
	5	2		6	9			
		4		1				
1		7	5	3				

Level 1

Puzzle 14

7			9		6			
		8	2				9	7
4	9	6		5	1			
		7		1	5		2	8
		5				3		
2	4		8	3		1		
			3	7		2	5	9
5	7				9	4		
			5		8			6

Level 1

Puzzle 15

	4		6	1				2
	7	6	8					
	5	3		2		9		8
4	2				6			3
	1	7				6	2	
6			1				4	7
3		4		6		7	1	
					4	2	8	
7				8	1		5	

Level 1

Puzzle 16

	9							2
		8	1	6		3	9	
	2	1	3			7		4
	5			4		8	3	
		9				2		
	6	7		3			5	
9		6			3	5	2	
	8	3		7	9	4		
5							7	

Level 1

Puzzle 17

		3		9				2
	8		2	7	4	3		
9				6				1
	7			8	5			4
3		5	7		9	1		6
2			1	4			7	
6				1				7
		4	6	3	7		2	
7				5		6		

Level 1

Puzzle 18

	9	7	4			5		
4	8	6			2			9
					9		3	8
7	6		9		8			3
	3						8	
2			1		6		7	4
6	2		8					
1			2			8	9	5
		9			5	3	2	

Level 1

Puzzle 19

5		9		3		7		4
	3			8	7		9	6
				2		1	3	
	4		5					7
			1	4	6			
9					3		6	
	2	5		1				
4	9		3	5			7	
3		7		6		8		9

Level 1

Puzzle 20

1	7			3	2	6		
9		2		6	5			1
	3					5		
		3	2			9		
8	9		3		6		5	2
		4			9	1		
		1					6	
7			6	5		2		3
		8	9	2			4	5

Level 1

Puzzle 21

	2	4			5	7		
1	6		8		3			5
3	9			1			6	2
		3						
	4	9	5		1	2	7	
						6		
4	8			9			2	7
9			1		8		4	6
		6	2			9	8	

Level 1

Puzzle 22

9	5		1				6	
	6				4	2		
	2			7	9			
4			5		2	8		1
	9	5	8		1	4	3	
3		8	9		7			6
			2	1			5	
		2	4				7	
	4				6		1	2

Level 1

Puzzle 23

	8	3						2
		9			3			5
7			9	8			4	1
	4	8	3	6	9			
		2				6		
			7	2	4	5	9	
1	3			9	8			6
6			4			7		
8						1	5	

Level 1

Puzzle 24

	9	8	7					1
7	4		3	8				
6						4		
		9		3		2	4	7
3			8	4	6			5
4	5	1		2		6		
		4						2
				5	8		3	4
2					3	7	6	

Level 1

Puzzle 25

5	4					8	7	3
			4					
3	7		1		5		2	
1	5				8	2		
	9	4		3		6	5	
		2	5				1	4
	3		7		6		4	5
					9			
6	1	7					3	2

Level 1

Puzzle 26

1			8	3			5	
		5				8		
2		4		9	5			
	3				4	9	7	
	5	8	7	2	1	3	6	
	1	7	3				2	
			6	5		1		3
		3				7		
	6			4	3			5

Level 1

Puzzle 27

3				9				7
	7					9		
4		6		8	7			
2		4	6	7				8
8	5		1	2	3		9	4
6				5	4	7		2
			9	4		2		6
		2					1	
7				6				9

Level 1

Puzzle 28

	9			7		3	8	
			8			9		
7	3	8	9	1				
1	2				9	6		
	6		5		2		4	
		4	6				5	2
				2	7	8	1	6
		3			8			
	7	6		9			2	

Level 1

Puzzle 29

	5	2	7		1	6		
	8		9	6	3	1		5
		1					9	7
1						3		
		8		1		5		
		6						2
2	6					7		
7		3	2	5	9		6	
		5	3		6	2	4	

Level 1

Puzzle 30

	8			7		3		
	9			1	3		2	7
3	7		2		8			
4			8	6				
	1	6				4	5	
				5	9			8
			5		2		1	3
1	2		7	3			8	
		3		8			7	

Level 1

Puzzle 31

	2		5		1		8	
						9	1	
7			9			6		2
			6	4		8	5	7
	7	4				3	2	
3	8	6		5	7			
2		7			8			3
	6	8						
	3		1		6		9	

Level 1

Puzzle 32

		9	3					2
3	8	7				4		9
		4		7			5	
		3		6	5	7	1	
8			7		3			4
	4	1	9	2		5		
	7			3		6		
6		8				2	4	5
1					6	3		

Level 1

Puzzle 33

		6	5				8	
3	1			8			7	5
	7		2		3			9
4		8			5			2
		3				8		
2			4			5		7
1			6		4		2	
5	2			1			3	4
	8				7	9		

Level 1

Puzzle 34

				5			9	
	4		3		7			8
	3		8					5
1	5	7				4		3
	8	4	1		3	2	5	
3		2				1	6	7
9					5		7	
8			6		2		1	
	2			8				

Level 1

Puzzle 35

	4	5	6			8		
6						9		3
8			1	2				7
		7	3	1	4	2		
			7		9			
		9	5	8	2	3		
3				5	7			8
9		2						1
		8			1	5	9	

Level 1

Puzzle 36

7	6		4		9		1	
4	8			3	7	6	9	
				8				5
8	5							7
	2						5	
9							6	4
3				4				
	1	7	8	9			2	3
	4		7		3		8	9

Level 1

Puzzle 37

				1			4	7
			3				1	
	9				7		5	
3	1		6			9	8	4
9	8	4				7	6	2
2	6	7			9		3	1
	4		1				9	
	2				6			
1	3			8				

Level 1

Puzzle 38

	3							
				7		9	8	4
9	7	8	2		1	3	5	6
	1		6	9		7		
			3		4			
		3		8	5		2	
4	9	6	1		8	5	3	7
3	8	1		5				
							1	

Level 1

Puzzle 39

8				5				
	7	1	4			9	8	
	6		8	2				
6		5		1		8	2	
	8	3		9		6	4	
	2	9		4		7		5
				6	2		5	
	9	7			3	4	1	
				7				8

Level 1

Puzzle 40

	1	7	8	3		5		2
8	3		9	2	5			
						9		3
1	5							7
6			4		1			5
2							4	6
7		5						
			1	5	2		7	9
4		1		7	9	3	5	

Level 1

Puzzle 41

						8	9	3
	8	6		9			7	1
					1			
	9	5	2	1				
3	7		8		4		1	9
				7	9	5	2	
			9					
4	1			6		3	5	
6	5	3						

LEVEL 2

Puzzle 42

1	9	2			8			
	6		3			7	2	
		8		4	6		5	
	4		7			6		
		3				2		
		1			3		7	
	5		9	1		4		
	1	7			5		6	
			4			5	3	1

Level 2

Puzzle 43

3			2					
		4		6	9			3
1				4		7		8
7	1				2	9		5
				3				
4		8	6				1	2
8		6		2				7
9			7	5		4		
					6			1

Level 2

Puzzle 44

			3		1		6	2
4	1		9		2	3	7	
			7					1
	8			9				
	7	5		2		6	3	
				3			2	
3					4			
	2	8	6		3		5	7
7	6		2		9			

Level 2

Puzzle 45

9					2			5
	3	5	7					8
			9					7
	7	4			5		6	
8		1	3		4	5		9
	9		8			3	2	
7					9			
2					7	9	4	
1			6					3

Level 2

Puzzle 46

2		3			6			8
	8					7		5
		7	5	3		2		4
9					5			
		1		7		6		
			1					3
8		9		1	4	3		
6		2					9	
3			8			4		7

Level 2

Puzzle 47

2						7	4	
5				1				9
		8					1	
	9		6	4		3	7	5
8		3				2		4
6	4	7		2	3		8	
	2					1		
3				5				6
	6	5						3

Level 2

Puzzle 48

		6				2	7	
9					2		3	8
			7				5	
8	5			9	6	1		
			2	3	8			
		2	5	1			4	3
	8				1			
4	1		6					9
	6	5				4		

Level 2

Puzzle 49

2				9	5			
	4				8			
	7			2	3		9	4
6				5				2
	2	4	9		6	7	3	
9				7				5
7	3		5	4			1	
			1				8	
			8	3				7

Level 2

Puzzle 50

		4						6
				7			1	
3	8		2					4
2	4			1	5		6	
1	9		6	4	2		7	3
	3		7	9			4	2
4					9		3	8
	1			6				
6						9		

Level 2

Puzzle 51

		2	3			1		
								8
6		1	7	2				
9		8		6		2	7	3
	1			3			4	
2	3	6		4		5		9
				7	2	3		4
1								
		3			8	6		

Level 2

Puzzle 52

					4			
		1			5	9	7	4
4		9	8			6	1	
3				5	7	2	4	
	7	4	2	3				8
	5	2			6	4		9
9	4	6	1			8		
			5					

Level 2

Puzzle 53

		4				6		
		8	2	3		7		9
	7	1	9					
5				7				6
	3		8	5	1		7	
8				2				1
					6	1	4	
7		9		8	2	3		
		5				2		

Level 2

Puzzle 54

			3		7		2	8
8		4			5			
5				9	6		4	
	9		7	3			1	
2				5				3
	5			6	8		9	
	3		5	1				2
			4			6		1
4	1		6		2			

Level 2

Puzzle 55

7	3				2	5	4	
	5	1	9		6	8		
		8				1		
8	1		5					
				3				
					7		1	6
		5				9		
		2	4		9	6	7	
	6	9	7				2	4

Level 2

Puzzle 56

	3		9	1	7	6		4
5					3			1
						9	7	
8			5			1		
1				8				6
		6			4			5
	6	5						
9			4					7
4		1	8	6	5		2	

Level 2

Puzzle 57

	1				4		5	6
7	8				5			
		6			7	3		
9	5				3	2	8	1
6	7	1	9				3	4
		3	1			6		
			5				2	3
4	2		7				1	

Level 2

Puzzle 58

1				3				
	8	7			1	6	4	
2					5		9	
		9	8	7	2			6
			3		6			
8			5	1	9	2		
	4		9					2
	7	5	4			8	1	
				6				5

Level 2

Puzzle 59

3		2		8			4	
7					5			8
				7		3	6	9
			9		4			5
		7		6		4		
1			2		7			
2	9	8		3				
6			5					1
	3			2		9		4

Level 2

Puzzle 60

8		7				5	3	
9		1	4			7		
			6	5		1		9
3				7				
4			5		6			7
				9				2
7		9		8	2			
		3			9	2		8
	2	8				9		1

Level 2

Puzzle 61

					7	8	2	
		2	6		5	9		
8	9	5			3			
7		3		4		5	1	
	2	9		1		4		3
			9			2	5	8
		7	5		2	6		
	5	4	8					

Level 2

Puzzle 62

	1			5				
		2	9	7		1		
6			2	1	8		7	
	5	4	8					3
	6						4	
3					7	6	5	
	2		7	9	5			1
		3		2	1	9		
				8			2	

Level 2

Puzzle 63

		7	1		5			
3			6	9				
			7		8		4	1
				5	4	8		
6	9	4				1	2	5
		3	2	1				
5	7		3		1			
				8	7			9
			4		9	2		

Level 2

Puzzle 64

9	2	1		8	7			
7				4				6
		4	3	5				
								5
8		6	1	2	4	3		9
4								
				1	5	8		
2				3				1
			8	9		6	3	4

Level 2

Puzzle 65

								6
2	3	6	7		4	5	8	
		7		1		3	9	
1	4				6	8		
				2				
		9	5				3	7
	6	4		3		9		
	5	3	1		7	4	6	2
8								

Level 2

Puzzle 66

5		9			6			
	3		2		8	6		
7		8		1	3			
	7			5	2			
		6		3		5		
			8	6			1	
			3	4		1		8
		2	6		5		3	
			1			4		6

Level 2

Puzzle 67

9	8	6	2			7		
					4			
5			9			6		
	2	4		1	5			
6			8	9	7			2
			3	4		5	7	
		3			1			5
			4					
		9			6	8	3	7

Level 2

Puzzle 68

9	4						6	
	5	2	9	8				1
				7	2			
		5	2		7			9
4			8		9			3
3			5		4	6		
			1	9				
1				4	5	7	3	
	3						9	6

Level 2

Puzzle 69

		1	4			2		5
6	4		8		3			
8	2		5					
1		3				6		
		7	3		9	5		
		2				3		8
					5		3	4
			9		8		5	6
7		6			4	8		

Level 2

Puzzle 70

				6	9		5	
		8						
6					2	3	9	8
2		7	9	1	6	8		5
9		1	4	5	8	2		3
5	7	9	6					2
						1		
	4		2	7				

Level 2

Puzzle 71

5		9					7	
		2	4			1	3	
4	8	1	6					5
					2	3		
3			1		4			7
		6	7					
8					7	9	1	3
	1	5			8	7		
	2					8		4

Level 2

Puzzle 72

		5	4					7
	4		7	6		3		2
				8		4		
	5		3	7	6		4	
	8						3	
	6		8	2	4		7	
		1		4				
8		2		1	9		5	
5					7	6		

Level 2

Puzzle 73

			6		2	4		
		7				8		1
		6			3		5	
	3		8		7	6		4
	9		2	1	6		3	
6		8	3		5		9	
	6		4			7		
5		3				1		
		2	5		8			

Level 2

Puzzle 74

1		9		8	4		6	
		5		1			3	
		6				7		
2	8					1		9
	9			4			8	
5		7					2	4
		3				2		
	4			5		8		
	1		9	2		4		7

Level 2

Puzzle 75

2					4		3	
			6	1		7		
	1			5		8	9	
		9	7					5
	3	8	5		6	2	1	
6					1	3		
	9	1		3			4	
		2		6	5			
	6		2					8

Level 2

Puzzle 76

9	5				8			
		8					1	
2	6			9	4	5	7	
		9	8					
4		7		5		1		3
					3	2		
	7	4	5	8			9	1
	9					3		
			6				4	7

Level 2

Puzzle 77

1	8			7			9	
	3				1	7		6
	5			3	2			8
3	2							
4			3		7			5
							6	4
7			1	5			3	
2		1	8				4	
	6			2			8	9

Level 2

Puzzle 78

	6				1	2		8
			5			1	3	
					6	9	4	7
	9	3	4				7	
	4						1	
	1				7	5	9	
4	3	1	8					
	8	9			4			
5		7	9				8	

Level 2

Puzzle 79

				7			4	
1	5			6	9			
9	4		2		8			1
6		4		3				5
	1						9	
8				2		4		3
7			5		4		1	6
			3	1			5	7
	2			8				

Level 2

Puzzle 80

						6		
	5		2	1			8	7
2	7			3	8		9	1
	6	5		2		7		
		1		8		9	4	
7	3		1	4			2	5
4	8			7	5		6	
		6						

Level 2

Puzzle 81

				2	7			
1	8					7		
					3	8	4	
5						1	3	9
3		7	1		4	5		8
9	1	6						4
	3	2	9					
		4					2	5
			6	3				

LEVEL 3

Puzzle 82

4				8			6	9
	3				4			5
	1			6			4	
				1	3		8	
	2	4				9	3	
	7		9	4				
	4			5			1	
7			6				5	
6	8			3				7

Level 3

Puzzle 83

	2	5						
	7		8			6	9	
8			2					
6	1		5		4			8
	4		7		8		2	
3			9		2		1	5
					5			9
	5	8			7		3	
						1	5	

Level 3

Puzzle 84

5			9		4			8
8					2	3		
	7		5					
	8		4		3			5
4		3				9		2
1			7		6		4	
					9		1	
		1	3					9
9			1		8			4

Level 3

Puzzle 85

			5			4		
4	1					5		
	2		3				6	
6			8		5		2	9
		1	6		2	7		
9	5		4		3			1
	3				4		5	
		9					7	3
		7			8			

Level 3

Puzzle 86

		6				2		4
			8				5	
					4	6	8	9
	5	7		8	6			
	8		5		3		2	
			4	2		8	9	
1	7	3	6					
	6				1			
4		9				1		

Level 3

Puzzle 87

					9			
1	6	8					9	
5		3			2		1	
				9	8	3	2	
8		7				9		1
	4	9	1	6				
	1		5			7		2
	2					5	4	9
			9					

Level 3

Puzzle 88

6			9			3		
						5		9
	9		6			7		1
8				2	7			6
9	4						7	2
7			5	1				4
3		9			6		8	
5		8						
		6			8			7

Level 3

Puzzle 89

				8	3			4
				4		5		9
1	5							6
		7	1		4			
4			9	5	8			3
			3		6	8		
3							6	8
5		1		6				
9			4	3				

Level 3

Puzzle 90

		6	3	1				5
						8		9
	1					4		
7	3	1	6	5				
9			7		3			6
				9	1	2	3	7
		7					8	
1		5						
2				8	4	3		

Level 3

Puzzle 91

1				3			5	
5	2		6	8				1
4			9				8	
9						7		
		6		1		8		
		5						6
	9				4			3
7				6	5		1	2
	5			2				8

Level 3

Puzzle 92

			4				8	2
6			5		7			1
	4		2	6				
3				8			9	
			1	5	3			
	5			4				8
				9	5		2	
7			8		1			3
1	6				4			

Level 3

Puzzle 93

	7		8			2		6
	3							
	1		2	4				
6			4		8	7		
4			1	3	6			9
		2	5		9			1
				8	7		6	
							8	
8		9			4		1	

Level 3

Puzzle 94

	5				1	4	2	
8								
7			9	5	8			
					6	7		
	2	3	4	8	7	1	5	
		9	5					
			2	6	4			7
								3
	1	5	3				4	

Level 3

Puzzle 95

1	3						5	
						2		8
	8	4	7	9				
2		1		8		4	3	
	5						8	
	6	9		2		5		1
				3	6	8	2	
6		7						
	2						1	5

Level 3

Puzzle 96

							3	4
		3	1					8
4			2			5		
			9		6		7	
2	3	7		4		6	9	1
	1		3		2			
		6			7			2
3					9	4		
5	4							

Level 3

Puzzle 97

		5	6				4	
		1		2	4	7		
				7		3	6	
		6	3			1		
		7		1		8		
		4			5	6		
	1	3		6				
		8	1	9		4		
	6				7	2		

Level 3

Puzzle 98

				3		8		4
5				8	6		2	3
	7							
			3					
1	9	3	2	7	5	4	6	8
					8			
							7	
6	4		5	9				2
7		9		6				

Level 3

Puzzle 99

		7	2	3			1	
			7	8				2
6								5
			5	7			4	8
2			1		8			3
1	5			9	4			
5								6
9				5	7			
	2			4	3	8		

Level 3

Puzzle 100

9		1			4		6	
8			1	6				
					3	5	8	
	4		7				3	8
	6						5	
2	1				5		7	
	9	3	5					
				1	9			6
	2		3			7		5

Level 3

Puzzle 101

9	4	1				3		
5	8		7		1	6		
7							1	
	1			4				
		5	9		6	4		
				8			2	
	6							1
		8	5		3		4	2
		3				9	6	8

Level 3

Puzzle 102

			5		6	1		
		6			2	4	7	
	8		4	1		3		
			2					4
	5			9			8	
2					4			
		7		3	8		5	
	9	1	6			2		
		3	7		1			

Level 3

Puzzle 103

		8		3	2	7		
				6			8	
	2		8			4	6	9
6					8	1		
		5				6		
		3	4					7
5	8	7			3		2	
	3			5				
		4	7	8		5		

Level 3

Puzzle 104

4		2			7			
1				3				
	7		2			4	6	
				2	3	9		1
3				7				4
7		8	5	1				
	8	6			9		5	
				5				2
			7			8		3

Level 3

Puzzle 105

4	8		3		6			
		5						
6	3	7			5	4		
	5						8	4
2		1				3		7
3	4						1	
		9	1			6	7	3
						2		
			6		3		9	1

Level 3

Puzzle 106

				4				
4		8			5	3		
6		7		1			8	
2				3	4			
1		5	7		9	2		4
			1	8				5
	6			7		5		1
		4	2			9		7
				9				

Level 3

Puzzle 107

			7					2
8		2		1		5		
				6	8			4
	8					3	5	6
7		4				2		8
5	2	6					7	
6			5	2				
		5		8		7		3
1					6			

Level 3

Puzzle 108

9	6		7				4	
5	4	3	1		9			2
1								
			5	1				
6				3				8
				9	6			
								4
8			9		4	1	3	5
	2				8		9	6

Level 3

Puzzle 109

1		3		9				7
				6	7	2		4
		7	8					
6				8	5	9		
			6		1			
		5	4	2				6
					4	8		
9		2	7	5				
8				3		5		9

Level 3

Puzzle 110

				9				3
		3	5					1
	6	8	3			7		
	2			5				
	5	9	7	6	3	4	8	
				1			5	
		7			4	6	9	
4					7	3		
6				8				

Level 3

Puzzle 111

							8	
		2		3			7	5
	7		9		6		1	
		7	3			5		
	5	3		4		8	2	
		6			9	1		
	6		4		1		9	
7	8			5		4		
	2							

Level 3

Puzzle 112

		7			6	2	1	
			4			6	7	
							5	
8				4	9	3		2
		1	3		2	5		
3		2	5	8				9
	9							
	2	8			1			
	5	6	2			4		

Level 3

Puzzle 113

		1		8				3
7	4		6			9		2
					2			
9	8		1			2		
6				3				4
		2			7		1	6
			7					
2		6			9		7	5
4				1		3		

Level 3

Puzzle 114

	9		5	4	6			7
		3						8
4						5		
7					5	4	8	2
			6		9			
1	2	5	7					3
		1						4
5						1		
8			9	1	7		3	

Level 3

Puzzle 115

		4		9		5	2	
			4		5			8
9			3			4		
7			1	8				
		3	2		4	9		
				6	7			4
		7			8			5
6			5		2			
	5	1		4		3		

Level 3

Puzzle 116

9			8	1			6	
	7							
3			7	9		5		
4		3	9	8				
8				3				6
				6	7	1		3
		1		4	8			9
							1	
	9			7	3			8

Level 3

Puzzle 117

	2	5		1				3
							8	5
3	1			5	9			
	5	9			2			
	3		1		6		2	
			5			4	6	
			2	8			9	4
1	8							
7				4		6	1	

Level 3

Puzzle 118

		7		1	6	5		
5	6		8				9	
4	1			3	9			6
8		5						
						2		9
3			2	5			8	4
	5				4		2	3
		1	7	8		9		

Level 3

Puzzle 119

					9	8		3
7		2				6	1	
				7			4	5
					3	9		7
			5	2	7			
5		1	9					
9	1			3				
	6	5				1		2
4		8	1					

Level 3

Puzzle 120

6						9		
7	4			5	6	3		
1			9		4		5	8
		6						9
3								4
2						8		
4	3		5		7			6
		7	3	2			9	5
		2						1

Level 3

Puzzle 121

					4	7		6
		4		7			9	
5			8				3	1
		2						5
			1		6			
3						2		
6	4				7			9
	8			5		3		
7		9	6					

LEVEL 4

Puzzle 122

			6	8	4			9
			5					
	9						3	8
2				7		6		3
	1						5	
6		8		1				7
4	6						9	
					6			
8			2	3	7			

Level 4

Puzzle 123

7							3	
2			7		1	6	8	
			9			7	2	
		4	5		2			
			6		7	1		
	4	2			9			
	9	1	2		4			5
	5							2

Level 4

Puzzle 124

	1		3					6
				2				3
		5	6				7	
		9	7		4		5	
	8			5			4	
	2		8		1	7		
	3				6	1		
6				9				
4					7		6	

Level 4

Puzzle 125

7		2					9	
		1	6	5				
6		3		8				
	3				9		2	
9				4				8
	7		2				1	
				1		4		5
				2	5	8		
	4					1		2

Level 4

Puzzle 126

4		1			7	6		2
		7					9	
8					3	1		
		9					1	
	2			8			7	
	1					3		
		3	5					4
	5					8		
1		4	2			7		6

Level 4

Puzzle 127

3		1	4			7		
					7	9	5	
		2	9					1
			8		1			
	6						2	
			3		6			
2					5	3		
	1	6	7					
		4			2	8		6

Level 4

Puzzle 128

		4				8		
					6	3	2	7
8						6		
			1		7		6	
7		3		5		1		2
	5		3		9			
		5						6
4	8	9	5					
		2				4		

Level 4

Puzzle 129

		6		7				
	2				1			
8			9			5		2
	4		6	1				9
	7			9			3	
9				5	4		7	
5		1			6			4
			7				8	
				3		6		

Level 4

Puzzle 130

				1	5	4		2
			9					
7		5				6		3
9				4			5	
		8		7		2		
	5			3				1
2		7				9		4
					1			
4		1	3	9				

Level 4

Puzzle 131

	5	9			1	2		8
				5	8			6
					4			
	6	4			2			
		1		4		5		
			1			7	4	
			4					
1			7	8				
8		5	3			1	7	

Level 4

Puzzle 132

6	9							
			2		7			8
	5			8	1	3		
5			6					
4	2			5			9	6
					9			1
		7	4	3			1	
2			5		6			
							2	7

Level 4

Puzzle 133

						5	1	
2			7					6
	7				5	4	9	
			2	1	3			
	9			4			2	
			9	8	6			
	2	8	6				7	
7					2			5
	1	9						

Level 4

Puzzle 134

			8	2	3	5		
8			5				2	
2	5							
	3	9			1			
	8						9	
			7			8	5	
							4	9
	6				9			7
		1	4	3	6			

Level 4

Puzzle 135

			2		8		9	6
	8	7		4				
						8		3
	3	6		9	7			
			8	1		3	2	
9		4						
				5		4	1	
8	2		4		1			

Level 4

Puzzle 136

6						1	4	
				3	4			8
		1	2					
	2		9	8	7	6		
		4	6	2	3		1	
					8	7		
8			4	5				
	5	3						2

Level 4

Puzzle 137

	9		7			1		4
5	8		6		1			
								9
	7			3	6	5		
				1				
		6	5	7			8	
2								
			8		5		4	2
4		7			3		9	

Level 4

Puzzle 138

						4		
	2		9			3	7	
		9	2	5				
8		2		6				4
			3		2			
6				7		2		1
				9	4	7		
	3	6			8		9	
		5						

Level 4

Puzzle 139

		7	8	9	2	1		
				4		2		
	6	1						
						7		9
	9	2				5	6	
3		8						
						3	2	
		4		5				
		5	2	8	7	9		

Level 4

Puzzle 140

	4		5					2
		2	8				5	
				2				4
		3	1		9		2	
	5						3	
	7		4		8	1		
3				7				
	8				1	6		
1					3		4	

Level 4

Puzzle 141

	2	5	7			3	6	
		3						
	9			4				8
				9	2	7		
2								4
		7	6	3				
3				8			4	
						5		
	4	6			5	1	7	

Level 4

Puzzle 142

		4	6		1		8	
				8				
		3			4		1	7
			3					
	4	7	1		8	3	6	
					7			
1	8		2			9		
				7				
	6		5		3	2		

Level 4

Puzzle 143

5	1		7				6	
		8						
2						5		9
	5		1		8			
	8	3				6	4	
			6		5		3	
7		4						1
						9		
	3				9		8	2

Level 4

Puzzle 144

2		1			9			7
			4	3				5
	8		5					1
	9		3	1				
				5	7		4	
7					3		9	
9				4	8			
4			6			1		3

Level 4

Puzzle 145

				7		5	6	
					4		7	
					6	9		8
			9	2		7		
	9	5		1		8	4	
		7		3	5			
3		2	8					
	7		5					
	5	8		4				

Level 4

Puzzle 146

		4		3		2	5	
			6				9	
	6			4		7		
6	9			1			3	
				6				
	3			7			8	4
		1		8			7	
	5				3			
	4	8		2		1		

Level 4

Puzzle 147

	4	6			9			
5						2		
							9	
7	1	9			4	3		
4			2		7			5
		2	3			7	4	6
	8							
		7						4
			6			5	8	

Level 4

Puzzle 148

7					1	4		
				5				
1	4		9					7
			1				8	4
8		5				7		9
2	7				5			
4					3		1	2
				6				
		3	4					8

Level 4

Puzzle 149

	5		8					7
4					9		2	6
				4				
5	8				1			
	9		7		2		1	
			9				3	4
				2				
3	7		5					8
2					3		9	

Level 4

Puzzle 150

						5		
2		9			3			7
5		4	1		8			
9	2							
	6	5				9	2	
							1	3
			5		4	8		9
6			7			4		2
		2						

Level 4

Puzzle 151

					3	7	5	
	2			6			1	
		1	4		8			9
		9			7		8	
	4		2			1		
7			3		6	8		
	5			8			2	
	9	3	7					

Level 4

Puzzle 152

	3			9				7
						4		
		6		3	4	5		8
	6	7			3			5
5			1			9	2	
9		5	3	6		1		
		8						
2				8			9	

Level 4

Puzzle 153

						9	6	3
	8	1	3		7	4		5
			2			8	9	
4				1				6
	7	5			6			
9		2	7		4	1	3	
5	1	8						

Level 4

Puzzle 154

		6	4		8		3	
	9		7					
		8			1			5
5			2			8		1
8		1			5			3
9			8			2		
					7		4	
	7		9		3	1		

Level 4

Puzzle 155

1		4	5					
7			1		8	3		
	2					4		
			6	8				5
4								6
2				9	5			
		1					4	
		5	9		6			8
					3	1		9

Level 4

Puzzle 156

				3	2			9
		2	8					
5		1			6	8	7	
								4
9			7	2	8			3
7								
	1	4	6			5		7
					7	6		
6			1	9				

Level 4

Puzzle 157

		6	3					1
		2					3	
		9			2			
		3		5				6
6		8	7	4	3	9		2
4				1		7		
			1			5		
	5					4		
8					6	3		

Level 4

Puzzle 158

	6					2		
							4	5
		4		5	7			3
	4				8			9
8		9		2		6		4
2			6				7	
9			2	4		8		
4	7							
		6					1	

Level 4

Puzzle 159

				4				
	9			7	8			
5		6				8	7	2
4				5			2	
	5			6			4	
	7			8				9
2	6	4				7		1
			7	2			5	
				9				

Level 4

Puzzle 160

	7		9			1	6	5
8	5		1			2		
		2		3			1	
3				4				8
	6			9		7		
		8			5		7	1
4	1	9			8		3	

Level 4

Puzzle 161

				3				8
	7		5					2
		2	4				9	
		5				2	7	
	9						1	
	8	1				5		
	6				2	1		
8					7		2	
7				9				

LEVEL 5

Puzzle 162

				5				
9			6					1
			2				3	5
	8	2	9			7		
			8		7			
		9			6	4	5	
8	4				9			
7					8			3
				1				

Level 5

Puzzle 163

		6		9		2	4	
5					8			
	7			4			3	
	9						7	
			1		2			
	3						1	
	4			7			9	
			6					1
	8	9		3		7		

Level 5

Puzzle 164

		2		8				
4		7			5			9
					1		2	
		4	7	3				
	8						1	
				4	9	5		
	9		8					
5			9			7		3
				6		4		

Level 5

Puzzle 165

	7	6			4			
			2			1		
1	2					3	5	
	3				7			
6								3
			5				2	
	5	4					1	8
		7			6			
			1			2	9	

Level 5

Puzzle 166

3	8				7			
	4	1		8				
		9	3			2		
5			6				3	
		6				5		
	2				4			8
		2			3	7		
				4		1	6	
			2				9	3

Level 5

Puzzle 167

			6	5	4			
2				7				5
	6				1	4		7
		1					3	
7								9
	2					1		
9		3	4				8	
5				9				2
			3	6	8			

Level 5

Puzzle 168

			1					2
			3	8	4	6		
	3			5		7		
	2				7			
9								5
			6				8	
		8		6			3	
		6	4	2	1			
4					9			

Level 5

Puzzle 169

6			2					5
		3	4		8			
		7	1				2	
9	6							
	2						1	
							7	2
	5				4	8		
			7		6	5		
8					3			9

Level 5

Puzzle 170

	9							
6			1			8	2	
		8	4			3	1	
			5	7				6
2				1	8			
	5	9			3	6		
	6	2			9			4
							8	

Level 5

Puzzle 171

				3	9			
6			5	1				
	5	1					4	8
	6	8	2					
					4	1	9	
3	2					9	1	
				6	1			5
			7	2				

Level 5

Puzzle 172

		7	6				3	
2				3		1	7	
	9							
5	8		2					
			8		9			
					5		9	4
							8	
	4	3		1				5
	5				4	9		

Level 5

Puzzle 173

6			8		5	7	1	
	4	2						
								6
		6		8	1			
	2						4	
			6	7		1		
2								
						5	9	
	3	8	1		6			7

Level 5

Puzzle 174

	4				1			8
7					2	5		
		2					9	
8			6					4
			9		4			
		5			3	7		
	6					2		
		1	8					6
5			1				8	

Level 5

Puzzle 175

	2				3			
		6				9	2	
			5		6			
4	3		7					1
		9		8		6		
1					4		9	7
			8		5			
	9	4				2		
			1				3	

Level 5

Puzzle 176

4					9	3		8
6				3			7	4
					1			
				9		6	5	
				5				
	7	1		2				
			5					
3	8			4				7
7		2	8					3

Level 5

Puzzle 177

5		1	9			4		7
								1
		6		8			3	
	2				3			
1								9
			7				5	
	8			6		9		
3								
7		9			1	5		4

Level 5

Puzzle 178

5	4		8					1
							2	
		8	6	4				
	8			9				4
		6		7		9		
2				5			1	
				6	3	8		
	6							
1					7		5	6

Level 5

Puzzle 179

6					8			
		8			2		6	
9	5	2					7	
					4	5		
8				6				4
		7	2					
	7					3	2	6
	8		7			4		
			9					8

Level 5

Puzzle 180

						9	2	
7		9	4				3	
			5	8				1
				3			9	
4								2
	2			7				
5				9	6			
	6				2	1		5
	1	3						

Level 5

Puzzle 181

8	6		9	3		2		
	4			8				
9								8
	3	7					5	
				6				
	5					1	7	
5								1
				9			4	
		8		2	3		6	9

Level 5

Puzzle 182

			1		5			
	7						8	
		2		9		4		
6			8		7			1
4				2				3
7			3		4			5
		9		4		2		
	8						3	
			7		6			

Level 5

Puzzle 183

				9	1	4		
		6		3				
5							9	
2		9			5	3		
7								6
		3	4			1		5
	8							1
				4		5		
		4	8	7				

Level 5

Puzzle 184

	3		9			7	1	
5						6		
6					1			3
	9			4	8			
				1				
			7	2			3	
4			3					8
		5						4
	1	2			7		9	

Level 5

Puzzle 185

1		3			9	7		
	7		5			2		6
				6				
	3					4	8	
				3				
	5	4					3	
				7				
9		1			5		6	
		6	2			3		5

Level 5

Puzzle 186

7		3	8				5	
			4					9
	2						3	8
3						1		5
				4				
1		8						7
5	7						8	
9					2			
	8				4	2		3

Level 5

Puzzle 187

		8			9		1	
			3					
	4			2	6			9
	2			4				
		3	1		8	2		
				7			3	
8			9	1			7	
					4			
	6		2			4		

Level 5

Puzzle 188

	1	3					6	
			9	5	3			
8				4	1			
		6			8			
3								4
			4			5		
			7	3				2
			8	1	6			
	4					7	1	

Level 5

Puzzle 189

		1	3				8	
		3	8				1	5
4								
	8	5		1			3	
				5				
	4			9		2	5	
								2
6	2				7	1		
	3				4	9		

Level 5

Puzzle 190

	7							
3			4			5	6	
		1	3			2	4	
		3	1					8
7					4	1		
	8	4			1	3		
	1	2			7			5
							2	

Level 5

Puzzle 191

5					6	3		
				8			9	4
		9						8
6				3			8	
	1						6	
	9			4				2
7						9		
9	5			2				
		2	4					3

Level 5

Puzzle 192

3								1
9					8			
	8	4	7	5		2		
		2				6		
1								4
		7				5		
		6		2	4	3	8	
			3					7
5								9

Level 5

Puzzle 193

7	3						6	
				1				
8		2	9	4			7	
				3	2			
		4				2		
			5	7				
	5			8	1	6		4
				2				
	6						5	3

Level 5

Puzzle 194

					9			
6	4		5			3		
	3				2			
		7			8		5	
9	5			4			3	6
	2		1			7		
			9				8	
		8			5		9	2
			7					

Level 5

Puzzle 195

	9			8			2	7
5		1						3
			9					4
		8						6
			6		4			
9						5		
8					9			
7						6		8
6	2			5			9	

Level 5

Puzzle 196

		6						
			6	9				5
2		3	4				9	
	2	8					5	1
3	1					8	2	
	5				1	2		8
8				2	3			
						6		

Level 5

Puzzle 197

7			2					
8	1						6	
					6	3	5	
		1						
	6	9	5		8	1	3	
						9		
	8	5	9					
	3						8	7
					4			5

Level 5

Puzzle 198

1	9	3				7		
7			9					
	4		2				9	
		8						1
			4	1	7			
3						6		
	2				9		4	
					8			6
		4				1	3	5

Level 5

Puzzle 199

9			6			3	4	
	4							
		6	3			1	2	
2					4	8		
				8				
		3	9					5
	2	1			9	7		
							6	
	6	5			7			1

Level 5

Puzzle 200

			8			3	2	
		6						5
1	8		5			9		
	9					5		
2				8				7
		4					6	
		1			2		3	4
9						1		
	7	2			6			

Level 5

Puzzle 201

		9						
	4	8			9			3
			7	8				9
			8			2	6	
		4				1		
	8	7			3			
7				2	4			
8			9			5	2	
						7		

Level 5

Solutions 1–12

1

2	1	6	8	5	3	4	7	9
3	8	5	9	4	7	1	2	6
4	7	9	1	2	6	3	8	5
5	3	8	2	9	1	7	6	4
9	6	1	7	3	4	8	5	2
7	4	2	6	8	5	9	3	1
1	2	3	5	7	9	6	4	8
8	9	7	4	6	2	5	1	3
6	5	4	3	1	8	2	9	7

2

6	9	7	2	5	8	1	4	3
3	1	2	6	7	4	8	5	9
4	8	5	1	3	9	7	2	6
8	2	1	3	9	6	5	7	4
5	3	4	8	1	7	6	9	2
7	6	9	5	4	2	3	1	8
1	5	8	4	2	3	9	6	7
2	7	6	9	8	5	4	3	1
9	4	3	7	6	1	2	8	5

3

5	2	1	6	8	3	7	4	9
9	8	4	7	5	2	6	3	1
6	7	3	4	1	9	5	8	2
8	3	6	9	2	1	4	5	7
7	1	9	8	4	5	2	6	3
2	4	5	3	7	6	1	9	8
3	5	8	2	6	7	9	1	4
1	9	2	5	3	4	8	7	6
4	6	7	1	9	8	3	2	5

4

5	9	3	6	7	8	2	4	1
4	6	7	2	3	1	5	8	9
8	2	1	4	9	5	7	6	3
6	4	5	9	2	3	1	7	8
3	7	2	1	8	4	9	5	6
1	8	9	7	5	6	3	2	4
2	1	8	3	6	7	4	9	5
7	3	6	5	4	9	8	1	2
9	5	4	8	1	2	6	3	7

5

2	6	4	1	9	7	8	3	5
8	7	5	3	2	6	9	4	1
3	9	1	5	4	8	6	2	7
1	5	2	6	7	4	3	9	8
9	3	7	8	1	2	5	6	4
6	4	8	9	5	3	7	1	2
4	2	3	7	6	5	1	8	9
7	1	6	2	8	9	4	5	3
5	8	9	4	3	1	2	7	6

6

8	6	2	1	5	3	4	9	7
1	9	5	7	8	4	6	2	3
7	4	3	9	6	2	8	1	5
3	8	4	6	2	1	5	7	9
2	7	6	8	9	5	1	3	4
9	5	1	4	3	7	2	6	8
5	2	9	3	1	8	7	4	6
4	3	8	2	7	6	9	5	1
6	1	7	5	4	9	3	8	2

7

7	3	8	9	4	2	1	5	6
9	2	1	5	6	3	7	4	8
5	6	4	8	1	7	9	3	2
2	1	5	3	8	6	4	7	9
3	8	7	1	9	4	6	2	5
4	9	6	7	2	5	8	1	3
8	4	2	6	3	1	5	9	7
6	7	3	4	5	9	2	8	1
1	5	9	2	7	8	3	6	4

8

6	2	1	8	4	7	5	9	3
3	4	8	1	9	5	6	7	2
5	9	7	2	3	6	1	4	8
9	3	2	6	5	4	7	8	1
7	1	6	3	8	9	2	5	4
8	5	4	7	1	2	9	3	6
2	6	3	5	7	8	4	1	9
1	7	9	4	2	3	8	6	5
4	8	5	9	6	1	3	2	7

9

7	6	9	1	3	4	2	5	8
4	3	8	2	5	7	1	6	9
1	5	2	8	6	9	3	4	7
3	8	5	4	2	6	7	9	1
9	4	7	5	1	8	6	2	3
6	2	1	7	9	3	5	8	4
8	1	3	6	4	5	9	7	2
2	7	6	9	8	1	4	3	5
5	9	4	3	7	2	8	1	6

10

3	8	1	2	6	7	5	9	4
6	5	2	9	4	1	3	7	8
4	7	9	5	3	8	6	2	1
7	9	6	1	8	4	2	5	3
8	4	3	7	5	2	9	1	6
1	2	5	3	9	6	4	8	7
2	3	8	6	7	5	1	4	9
5	6	7	4	1	9	8	3	2
9	1	4	8	2	3	7	6	5

11

1	7	3	9	6	5	2	4	8
9	2	5	8	4	1	7	6	3
8	4	6	3	2	7	5	1	9
4	6	1	5	7	3	8	9	2
3	8	9	2	1	6	4	5	7
2	5	7	4	9	8	6	3	1
6	9	8	7	3	4	1	2	5
7	3	4	1	5	2	9	8	6
5	1	2	6	8	9	3	7	4

12

4	3	2	1	7	6	9	8	5
1	8	9	4	3	5	2	6	7
5	7	6	9	2	8	1	3	4
3	4	5	7	1	9	8	2	6
2	1	7	6	8	4	5	9	3
6	9	8	3	5	2	4	7	1
7	2	3	8	4	1	6	5	9
9	5	1	2	6	7	3	4	8
8	6	4	5	9	3	7	1	2

Solutions 13–24

13

4	7	1	9	2	3	5	6	8
5	3	8	7	4	6	9	1	2
6	2	9	8	5	1	7	3	4
7	4	6	1	8	5	2	9	3
8	9	5	3	7	2	6	4	1
2	1	3	6	9	4	8	7	5
3	5	2	4	6	9	1	8	7
9	8	4	2	1	7	3	5	6
1	6	7	5	3	8	4	2	9

14

7	2	3	9	8	6	5	4	1
1	5	8	2	4	3	6	9	7
4	9	6	7	5	1	8	3	2
3	6	7	4	1	5	9	2	8
8	1	5	6	9	2	3	7	4
2	4	9	8	3	7	1	6	5
6	8	1	3	7	4	2	5	9
5	7	2	1	6	9	4	8	3
9	3	4	5	2	8	7	1	6

15

8	4	9	6	1	3	5	7	2
2	7	6	8	5	9	4	3	1
1	5	3	4	2	7	9	6	8
4	2	8	5	7	6	1	9	3
9	1	7	3	4	8	6	2	5
6	3	5	1	9	2	8	4	7
3	8	4	2	6	5	7	1	9
5	9	1	7	3	4	2	8	6
7	6	2	9	8	1	3	5	4

16

3	9	5	7	8	4	6	1	2
7	4	8	1	6	2	3	9	5
6	2	1	3	9	5	7	8	4
1	5	2	9	4	7	8	3	6
8	3	9	6	5	1	2	4	7
4	6	7	2	3	8	1	5	9
9	7	6	4	1	3	5	2	8
2	8	3	5	7	9	4	6	1
5	1	4	8	2	6	9	7	3

17

4	6	3	8	9	1	7	5	2
5	8	1	2	7	4	3	6	9
9	2	7	5	6	3	8	4	1
1	7	6	3	8	5	2	9	4
3	4	5	7	2	9	1	8	6
2	9	8	1	4	6	5	7	3
6	5	2	9	1	8	4	3	7
8	1	4	6	3	7	9	2	5
7	3	9	4	5	2	6	1	8

18

3	9	7	4	8	1	5	6	2
4	8	6	3	5	2	7	1	9
5	1	2	6	7	9	4	3	8
7	6	1	9	4	8	2	5	3
9	3	4	5	2	7	6	8	1
2	5	8	1	3	6	9	7	4
6	2	5	8	9	3	1	4	7
1	7	3	2	6	4	8	9	5
8	4	9	7	1	5	3	2	6

19

5	8	9	6	3	1	7	2	4
1	3	2	4	8	7	5	9	6
7	6	4	9	2	5	1	3	8
6	4	8	5	9	2	3	1	7
2	7	3	1	4	6	9	8	5
9	5	1	8	7	3	4	6	2
8	2	5	7	1	9	6	4	3
4	9	6	3	5	8	2	7	1
3	1	7	2	6	4	8	5	9

20

1	7	5	8	3	2	6	9	4
9	8	2	4	6	5	3	7	1
4	3	6	1	9	7	5	2	8
5	1	3	2	7	4	9	8	6
8	9	7	3	1	6	4	5	2
6	2	4	5	8	9	1	3	7
2	5	1	7	4	3	8	6	9
7	4	9	6	5	8	2	1	3
3	6	8	9	2	1	7	4	5

21

8	2	4	9	6	5	7	1	3
1	6	7	8	2	3	4	9	5
3	9	5	4	1	7	8	6	2
2	7	3	6	8	9	1	5	4
6	4	9	5	3	1	2	7	8
5	1	8	7	4	2	6	3	9
4	8	1	3	9	6	5	2	7
9	5	2	1	7	8	3	4	6
7	3	6	2	5	4	9	8	1

22

9	5	4	1	2	8	7	6	3
7	6	1	3	5	4	2	8	9
8	2	3	6	7	9	1	4	5
4	7	6	5	3	2	8	9	1
2	9	5	8	6	1	4	3	7
3	1	8	9	4	7	5	2	6
6	8	7	2	1	3	9	5	4
1	3	2	4	9	5	6	7	8
5	4	9	7	8	6	3	1	2

23

4	8	3	1	5	7	9	6	2
2	1	9	6	4	3	8	7	5
7	5	6	9	8	2	3	4	1
5	4	8	3	6	9	2	1	7
9	7	2	8	1	5	6	3	4
3	6	1	7	2	4	5	9	8
1	3	7	5	9	8	4	2	6
6	2	5	4	3	1	7	8	9
8	9	4	2	7	6	1	5	3

24

5	9	8	7	6	4	3	2	1
7	4	2	3	8	1	5	9	6
6	1	3	5	9	2	4	7	8
8	6	9	1	3	5	2	4	7
3	2	7	8	4	6	9	1	5
4	5	1	9	2	7	6	8	3
1	3	4	6	7	9	8	5	2
9	7	6	2	5	8	1	3	4
2	8	5	4	1	3	7	6	9

Solutions 25–36

25

5	4	1	9	6	2	8	7	3
2	8	9	4	7	3	5	6	1
3	7	6	1	8	5	4	2	9
1	5	3	6	4	8	2	9	7
7	9	4	2	3	1	6	5	8
8	6	2	5	9	7	3	1	4
9	3	8	7	2	6	1	4	5
4	2	5	3	1	9	7	8	6
6	1	7	8	5	4	9	3	2

26

1	7	6	8	3	2	4	5	9
3	9	5	4	7	6	8	1	2
2	8	4	1	9	5	6	3	7
6	3	2	5	8	4	9	7	1
9	5	8	7	2	1	3	6	4
4	1	7	3	6	9	5	2	8
8	2	9	6	5	7	1	4	3
5	4	3	2	1	8	7	9	6
7	6	1	9	4	3	2	8	5

27

3	2	1	5	9	6	8	4	7
5	7	8	4	1	2	9	6	3
4	9	6	3	8	7	5	2	1
2	3	4	6	7	9	1	5	8
8	5	7	1	2	3	6	9	4
6	1	9	8	5	4	7	3	2
1	8	3	9	4	5	2	7	6
9	6	2	7	3	8	4	1	5
7	4	5	2	6	1	3	8	9

28

5	9	1	2	7	6	3	8	4
6	4	2	8	5	3	9	7	1
7	3	8	9	1	4	2	6	5
1	2	5	7	4	9	6	3	8
3	6	7	5	8	2	1	4	9
9	8	4	6	3	1	7	5	2
4	5	9	3	2	7	8	1	6
2	1	3	4	6	8	5	9	7
8	7	6	1	9	5	4	2	3

29

9	5	2	7	4	1	6	3	8
4	8	7	9	6	3	1	2	5
6	3	1	8	2	5	4	9	7
1	2	4	5	9	7	3	8	6
3	9	8	6	1	2	5	7	4
5	7	6	4	3	8	9	1	2
2	6	9	1	8	4	7	5	3
7	4	3	2	5	9	8	6	1
8	1	5	3	7	6	2	4	9

30

6	8	2	9	7	5	3	4	1
5	9	4	6	1	3	8	2	7
3	7	1	2	4	8	5	9	6
4	5	9	8	6	1	7	3	2
8	1	6	3	2	7	4	5	9
2	3	7	4	5	9	1	6	8
7	4	8	5	9	2	6	1	3
1	2	5	7	3	6	9	8	4
9	6	3	1	8	4	2	7	5

31

6	2	9	5	3	1	7	8	4
8	4	3	7	6	2	9	1	5
7	5	1	9	8	4	6	3	2
1	9	2	6	4	3	8	5	7
5	7	4	8	1	9	3	2	6
3	8	6	2	5	7	1	4	9
2	1	7	4	9	8	5	6	3
9	6	8	3	2	5	4	7	1
4	3	5	1	7	6	2	9	8

32

5	6	9	3	8	4	1	7	2
3	8	7	2	5	1	4	6	9
2	1	4	6	7	9	8	5	3
9	2	3	4	6	5	7	1	8
8	5	6	7	1	3	9	2	4
7	4	1	9	2	8	5	3	6
4	7	5	8	3	2	6	9	1
6	3	8	1	9	7	2	4	5
1	9	2	5	4	6	3	8	7

33

9	4	6	5	7	1	2	8	3
3	1	2	9	8	6	4	7	5
8	7	5	2	4	3	1	6	9
4	9	8	7	6	5	3	1	2
7	5	3	1	9	2	8	4	6
2	6	1	4	3	8	5	9	7
1	3	9	6	5	4	7	2	8
5	2	7	8	1	9	6	3	4
6	8	4	3	2	7	9	5	1

34

7	6	8	2	5	4	3	9	1
5	4	9	3	1	7	6	2	8
2	3	1	8	6	9	7	4	5
1	5	7	9	2	6	4	8	3
6	8	4	1	7	3	2	5	9
3	9	2	5	4	8	1	6	7
9	1	6	4	3	5	8	7	2
8	7	3	6	9	2	5	1	4
4	2	5	7	8	1	9	3	6

35

7	4	5	6	9	3	8	1	2
6	2	1	4	7	8	9	5	3
8	9	3	1	2	5	6	4	7
5	8	7	3	1	4	2	6	9
2	3	4	7	6	9	1	8	5
1	6	9	5	8	2	3	7	4
3	1	6	9	5	7	4	2	8
9	5	2	8	4	6	7	3	1
4	7	8	2	3	1	5	9	6

36

7	6	2	4	5	9	3	1	8
4	8	5	1	3	7	6	9	2
1	3	9	6	8	2	7	4	5
8	5	1	9	6	4	2	3	7
6	2	4	3	7	8	9	5	1
9	7	3	5	2	1	8	6	4
3	9	8	2	4	5	1	7	6
5	1	7	8	9	6	4	2	3
2	4	6	7	1	3	5	8	9

Solutions 37–48

37

6	5	3	9	1	8	2	4	7
8	7	2	3	5	4	6	1	9
4	9	1	2	6	7	3	5	8
3	1	5	6	7	2	9	8	4
9	8	4	5	3	1	7	6	2
2	6	7	8	4	9	5	3	1
7	4	6	1	2	3	8	9	5
5	2	8	4	9	6	1	7	3
1	3	9	7	8	5	4	2	6

38

5	3	4	8	6	9	2	7	1
1	6	2	5	7	3	9	8	4
9	7	8	2	4	1	3	5	6
8	1	5	6	9	2	7	4	3
7	2	9	3	1	4	8	6	5
6	4	3	7	8	5	1	2	9
4	9	6	1	2	8	5	3	7
3	8	1	4	5	7	6	9	2
2	5	7	9	3	6	4	1	8

39

8	3	2	7	5	9	1	6	4
5	7	1	4	3	6	9	8	2
9	6	4	8	2	1	5	7	3
6	4	5	3	1	7	8	2	9
7	8	3	2	9	5	6	4	1
1	2	9	6	4	8	7	3	5
4	1	8	9	6	2	3	5	7
2	9	7	5	8	3	4	1	6
3	5	6	1	7	4	2	9	8

40

9	1	7	8	3	4	5	6	2
8	3	6	9	2	5	7	1	4
5	4	2	7	1	6	9	8	3
1	5	4	2	6	3	8	9	7
6	7	9	4	8	1	2	3	5
2	8	3	5	9	7	1	4	6
7	9	5	3	4	8	6	2	1
3	6	8	1	5	2	4	7	9
4	2	1	6	7	9	3	5	8

41

5	4	1	6	2	7	8	9	3
2	8	6	5	9	3	4	7	1
9	3	7	4	8	1	2	6	5
8	9	5	2	1	6	7	3	4
3	7	2	8	5	4	6	1	9
1	6	4	3	7	9	5	2	8
7	2	8	9	3	5	1	4	6
4	1	9	7	6	8	3	5	2
6	5	3	1	4	2	9	8	7

42

1	9	2	5	7	8	3	4	6
5	6	4	3	9	1	7	2	8
7	3	8	2	4	6	1	5	9
8	4	5	7	2	9	6	1	3
6	7	3	1	8	4	2	9	5
9	2	1	6	5	3	8	7	4
3	5	6	9	1	2	4	8	7
4	1	7	8	3	5	9	6	2
2	8	9	4	6	7	5	3	1

43

3	8	5	2	1	7	6	4	9
2	7	4	8	6	9	1	5	3
1	6	9	5	4	3	7	2	8
7	1	3	4	8	2	9	6	5
6	5	2	9	3	1	8	7	4
4	9	8	6	7	5	3	1	2
8	3	6	1	2	4	5	9	7
9	2	1	7	5	8	4	3	6
5	4	7	3	9	6	2	8	1

44

5	9	7	3	4	1	8	6	2
4	1	6	9	8	2	3	7	5
8	3	2	7	6	5	9	4	1
2	8	3	5	9	6	7	1	4
1	7	5	4	2	8	6	3	9
6	4	9	1	3	7	5	2	8
3	5	1	8	7	4	2	9	6
9	2	8	6	1	3	4	5	7
7	6	4	2	5	9	1	8	3

45

9	1	7	4	8	2	6	3	5
4	3	5	7	1	6	2	9	8
6	8	2	9	5	3	4	1	7
3	7	4	2	9	5	8	6	1
8	2	1	3	6	4	5	7	9
5	9	6	8	7	1	3	2	4
7	6	3	5	4	9	1	8	2
2	5	8	1	3	7	9	4	6
1	4	9	6	2	8	7	5	3

46

2	5	3	7	4	6	9	1	8
4	8	6	9	2	1	7	3	5
1	9	7	5	3	8	2	6	4
9	3	4	6	8	5	1	7	2
5	2	1	4	7	3	6	8	9
7	6	8	1	9	2	5	4	3
8	7	9	2	1	4	3	5	6
6	4	2	3	5	7	8	9	1
3	1	5	8	6	9	4	2	7

47

2	1	6	9	3	5	7	4	8
5	7	4	8	1	2	6	3	9
9	3	8	7	6	4	5	1	2
1	9	2	6	4	8	3	7	5
8	5	3	1	7	9	2	6	4
6	4	7	5	2	3	9	8	1
4	2	9	3	8	6	1	5	7
3	8	1	2	5	7	4	9	6
7	6	5	4	9	1	8	2	3

48

5	3	6	9	8	4	2	7	1
9	7	4	1	5	2	6	3	8
1	2	8	7	6	3	9	5	4
8	5	3	4	9	6	1	2	7
7	4	1	2	3	8	5	9	6
6	9	2	5	1	7	8	4	3
2	8	9	3	4	1	7	6	5
4	1	7	6	2	5	3	8	9
3	6	5	8	7	9	4	1	2

Solutions 49-60

49

2	6	1	4	9	5	3	7	8
3	4	9	7	1	8	2	5	6
8	7	5	6	2	3	1	9	4
6	8	7	3	5	1	9	4	2
5	2	4	9	8	6	7	3	1
9	1	3	2	7	4	8	6	5
7	3	8	5	4	2	6	1	9
4	9	2	1	6	7	5	8	3
1	5	6	8	3	9	4	2	7

50

7	5	4	9	3	1	2	8	6
9	6	2	8	7	4	3	1	5
3	8	1	2	5	6	7	9	4
2	4	7	3	1	5	8	6	9
1	9	8	6	4	2	5	7	3
5	3	6	7	9	8	1	4	2
4	7	5	1	2	9	6	3	8
8	1	9	5	6	3	4	2	7
6	2	3	4	8	7	9	5	1

51

4	9	2	3	8	5	1	6	7
3	7	5	9	1	6	4	2	8
6	8	1	7	2	4	9	3	5
9	4	8	5	6	1	2	7	3
5	1	7	2	3	9	8	4	6
2	3	6	8	4	7	5	1	9
8	6	9	1	7	2	3	5	4
1	5	4	6	9	3	7	8	2
7	2	3	4	5	8	6	9	1

52

5	6	7	9	1	4	3	8	2
8	2	1	3	6	5	9	7	4
4	3	9	8	7	2	6	1	5
3	9	8	6	5	7	2	4	1
2	1	5	4	9	8	7	6	3
6	7	4	2	3	1	5	9	8
1	5	2	7	8	6	4	3	9
9	4	6	1	2	3	8	5	7
7	8	3	5	4	9	1	2	6

53

9	2	4	7	1	5	6	8	3
6	5	8	2	3	4	7	1	9
3	7	1	9	6	8	5	2	4
5	1	2	4	7	9	8	3	6
4	3	6	8	5	1	9	7	2
8	9	7	6	2	3	4	5	1
2	8	3	5	9	6	1	4	7
7	4	9	1	8	2	3	6	5
1	6	5	3	4	7	2	9	8

54

1	6	9	3	4	7	5	2	8
8	7	4	1	2	5	9	3	6
5	2	3	8	9	6	1	4	7
6	9	8	7	3	4	2	1	5
2	4	7	9	5	1	8	6	3
3	5	1	2	6	8	7	9	4
7	3	6	5	1	9	4	8	2
9	8	2	4	7	3	6	5	1
4	1	5	6	8	2	3	7	9

55

7	3	6	1	8	2	5	4	9
2	5	1	9	4	6	8	3	7
9	4	8	3	7	5	1	6	2
8	1	7	5	6	4	2	9	3
6	9	4	2	3	1	7	5	8
5	2	3	8	9	7	4	1	6
4	7	5	6	2	3	9	8	1
3	8	2	4	1	9	6	7	5
1	6	9	7	5	8	3	2	4

56

2	3	8	9	1	7	6	5	4
5	9	7	6	4	3	2	8	1
6	1	4	2	5	8	9	7	3
8	4	3	5	7	6	1	9	2
1	5	9	3	8	2	7	4	6
7	2	6	1	9	4	8	3	5
3	6	5	7	2	9	4	1	8
9	8	2	4	3	1	5	6	7
4	7	1	8	6	5	3	2	9

57

3	1	2	8	9	4	7	5	6
7	8	9	3	6	5	1	4	2
5	4	6	2	1	7	3	9	8
9	5	4	6	7	3	2	8	1
2	3	8	4	5	1	9	6	7
6	7	1	9	2	8	5	3	4
8	9	3	1	4	2	6	7	5
1	6	7	5	8	9	4	2	3
4	2	5	7	3	6	8	1	9

58

1	9	6	7	3	4	5	2	8
5	8	7	2	9	1	6	4	3
2	3	4	6	8	5	1	9	7
4	1	9	8	7	2	3	5	6
7	5	2	3	4	6	9	8	1
8	6	3	5	1	9	2	7	4
3	4	1	9	5	8	7	6	2
6	7	5	4	2	3	8	1	9
9	2	8	1	6	7	4	3	5

59

3	1	2	6	8	9	5	4	7
7	6	9	3	4	5	1	2	8
4	8	5	1	7	2	3	6	9
8	2	3	9	1	4	6	7	5
9	5	7	8	6	3	4	1	2
1	4	6	2	5	7	8	9	3
2	9	8	4	3	1	7	5	6
6	7	4	5	9	8	2	3	1
5	3	1	7	2	6	9	8	4

60

8	6	7	9	2	1	5	3	4
9	5	1	4	3	8	7	2	6
2	3	4	6	5	7	1	8	9
3	9	6	2	7	4	8	1	5
4	8	2	5	1	6	3	9	7
1	7	5	8	9	3	4	6	2
7	4	9	1	8	2	6	5	3
5	1	3	7	6	9	2	4	8
6	2	8	3	4	5	9	7	1

Solutions 61-72

61

3	4	6	1	9	7	8	2	5
1	7	2	6	8	5	9	3	4
8	9	5	4	2	3	1	7	6
7	6	3	2	4	8	5	1	9
4	1	8	3	5	9	7	6	2
5	2	9	7	1	6	4	8	3
6	3	1	9	7	4	2	5	8
9	8	7	5	3	2	6	4	1
2	5	4	8	6	1	3	9	7

62

7	1	8	3	5	4	2	9	6
4	3	2	9	7	6	1	8	5
6	9	5	2	1	8	3	7	4
2	5	4	8	6	9	7	1	3
1	6	7	5	3	2	8	4	9
3	8	9	1	4	7	6	5	2
8	2	6	7	9	5	4	3	1
5	7	3	4	2	1	9	6	8
9	4	1	6	8	3	5	2	7

63

9	8	7	1	4	5	6	3	2
3	4	1	6	9	2	5	7	8
2	6	5	7	3	8	9	4	1
7	1	2	9	5	4	8	6	3
6	9	4	8	7	3	1	2	5
8	5	3	2	1	6	7	9	4
5	7	9	3	2	1	4	8	6
4	2	6	5	8	7	3	1	9
1	3	8	4	6	9	2	5	7

64

9	2	1	6	8	7	4	5	3
7	3	5	2	4	1	9	8	6
6	8	4	3	5	9	7	1	2
1	7	3	9	6	8	2	4	5
8	5	6	1	2	4	3	7	9
4	9	2	5	7	3	1	6	8
3	6	9	4	1	5	8	2	7
2	4	8	7	3	6	5	9	1
5	1	7	8	9	2	6	3	4

65

4	9	1	8	5	3	2	7	6
2	3	6	7	9	4	5	8	1
5	8	7	6	1	2	3	9	4
1	4	5	3	7	6	8	2	9
3	7	8	9	2	1	6	4	5
6	2	9	5	4	8	1	3	7
7	6	4	2	3	5	9	1	8
9	5	3	1	8	7	4	6	2
8	1	2	4	6	9	7	5	3

66

5	2	9	4	7	6	3	8	1
1	3	4	2	9	8	6	7	5
7	6	8	5	1	3	2	4	9
3	7	1	9	5	2	8	6	4
8	4	6	7	3	1	5	9	2
2	9	5	8	6	4	7	1	3
6	5	7	3	4	9	1	2	8
4	1	2	6	8	5	9	3	7
9	8	3	1	2	7	4	5	6

67

9	8	6	2	5	3	7	1	4
3	7	2	1	6	4	9	5	8
5	4	1	9	7	8	6	2	3
7	2	4	6	1	5	3	8	9
6	3	5	8	9	7	1	4	2
1	9	8	3	4	2	5	7	6
2	6	3	7	8	1	4	9	5
8	5	7	4	3	9	2	6	1
4	1	9	5	2	6	8	3	7

68

9	4	8	3	5	1	2	6	7
7	5	2	9	8	6	3	4	1
6	1	3	4	7	2	9	8	5
8	6	5	2	3	7	4	1	9
4	2	1	8	6	9	5	7	3
3	9	7	5	1	4	6	2	8
2	7	6	1	9	3	8	5	4
1	8	9	6	4	5	7	3	2
5	3	4	7	2	8	1	9	6

69

3	7	1	4	9	6	2	8	5
6	4	5	8	2	3	9	1	7
8	2	9	5	1	7	4	6	3
1	8	3	7	5	2	6	4	9
4	6	7	3	8	9	5	2	1
5	9	2	6	4	1	3	7	8
9	1	8	2	6	5	7	3	4
2	3	4	9	7	8	1	5	6
7	5	6	1	3	4	8	9	2

70

4	2	3	8	6	9	7	5	1
7	9	8	1	3	5	6	2	4
6	1	5	7	4	2	3	9	8
2	3	7	9	1	6	8	4	5
8	5	4	3	2	7	9	1	6
9	6	1	4	5	8	2	7	3
5	7	9	6	8	1	4	3	2
3	8	2	5	9	4	1	6	7
1	4	6	2	7	3	5	8	9

71

5	3	9	2	8	1	4	7	6
6	7	2	4	9	5	1	3	8
4	8	1	6	7	3	2	9	5
1	5	7	8	6	2	3	4	9
3	9	8	1	5	4	6	2	7
2	4	6	7	3	9	5	8	1
8	6	4	5	2	7	9	1	3
9	1	5	3	4	8	7	6	2
7	2	3	9	1	6	8	5	4

72

3	1	5	4	9	2	8	6	7
9	4	8	7	6	5	3	1	2
7	2	6	1	8	3	4	9	5
2	5	9	3	7	6	1	4	8
4	8	7	9	5	1	2	3	6
1	6	3	8	2	4	5	7	9
6	7	1	5	4	8	9	2	3
8	3	2	6	1	9	7	5	4
5	9	4	2	3	7	6	8	1

Solutions 73–84

73

9	5	1	6	8	2	4	7	3
3	2	7	9	5	4	8	6	1
4	8	6	1	7	3	9	5	2
2	3	5	8	9	7	6	1	4
7	9	4	2	1	6	5	3	8
6	1	8	3	4	5	2	9	7
8	6	9	4	3	1	7	2	5
5	4	3	7	2	9	1	8	6
1	7	2	5	6	8	3	4	9

74

1	3	9	7	8	4	5	6	2
4	7	5	6	1	2	9	3	8
8	2	6	5	3	9	7	4	1
2	8	4	3	6	5	1	7	9
3	9	1	2	4	7	6	8	5
5	6	7	8	9	1	3	2	4
9	5	3	4	7	8	2	1	6
7	4	2	1	5	6	8	9	3
6	1	8	9	2	3	4	5	7

75

2	8	6	9	7	4	5	3	1
9	5	3	6	1	8	7	2	4
7	1	4	3	5	2	8	9	6
1	2	9	7	8	3	4	6	5
4	3	8	5	9	6	2	1	7
6	7	5	4	2	1	3	8	9
5	9	1	8	3	7	6	4	2
8	4	2	1	6	5	9	7	3
3	6	7	2	4	9	1	5	8

76

9	5	1	2	7	8	4	3	6
7	4	8	3	6	5	9	1	2
2	6	3	1	9	4	5	7	8
6	3	9	8	2	1	7	5	4
4	2	7	9	5	6	1	8	3
1	8	5	7	4	3	2	6	9
3	7	4	5	8	2	6	9	1
8	9	6	4	1	7	3	2	5
5	1	2	6	3	9	8	4	7

77

1	8	4	5	7	6	2	9	3
9	3	2	4	8	1	7	5	6
6	5	7	9	3	2	4	1	8
3	2	5	6	4	8	9	7	1
4	1	6	3	9	7	8	2	5
8	7	9	2	1	5	3	6	4
7	4	8	1	5	9	6	3	2
2	9	1	8	6	3	5	4	7
5	6	3	7	2	4	1	8	9

78

3	6	4	7	9	1	2	5	8
9	7	2	5	4	8	1	3	6
1	5	8	2	3	6	9	4	7
8	9	3	4	1	5	6	7	2
7	4	5	6	2	9	8	1	3
2	1	6	3	8	7	5	9	4
4	3	1	8	5	2	7	6	9
6	8	9	1	7	4	3	2	5
5	2	7	9	6	3	4	8	1

79

2	8	6	1	7	3	5	4	9
1	5	7	4	6	9	3	8	2
9	4	3	2	5	8	6	7	1
6	9	4	8	3	7	1	2	5
3	1	2	6	4	5	7	9	8
8	7	5	9	2	1	4	6	3
7	3	8	5	9	4	2	1	6
4	6	9	3	1	2	8	5	7
5	2	1	7	8	6	9	3	4

80

1	9	8	7	5	4	6	3	2
6	5	3	2	1	9	4	8	7
2	7	4	6	3	8	5	9	1
9	6	5	4	2	3	7	1	8
8	4	7	9	6	1	2	5	3
3	2	1	5	8	7	9	4	6
7	3	9	1	4	6	8	2	5
4	8	2	3	7	5	1	6	9
5	1	6	8	9	2	3	7	4

81

4	6	5	8	2	7	9	1	3
1	8	3	4	6	9	7	5	2
2	7	9	5	1	3	8	4	6
5	4	8	2	7	6	1	3	9
3	2	7	1	9	4	5	6	8
9	1	6	3	5	8	2	7	4
7	3	2	9	4	5	6	8	1
6	9	4	7	8	1	3	2	5
8	5	1	6	3	2	4	9	7

82

4	5	7	3	8	2	1	6	9
2	3	6	1	9	4	8	7	5
9	1	8	5	6	7	3	4	2
5	6	9	2	1	3	7	8	4
1	2	4	8	7	5	9	3	6
8	7	3	9	4	6	5	2	1
3	4	2	7	5	9	6	1	8
7	9	1	6	2	8	4	5	3
6	8	5	4	3	1	2	9	7

83

9	2	5	3	4	6	7	8	1
4	7	3	8	5	1	6	9	2
8	6	1	2	7	9	5	4	3
6	1	2	5	3	4	9	7	8
5	4	9	7	1	8	3	2	6
3	8	7	9	6	2	4	1	5
7	3	4	1	2	5	8	6	9
1	5	8	6	9	7	2	3	4
2	9	6	4	8	3	1	5	7

84

5	1	6	9	3	4	7	2	8
8	9	4	6	7	2	3	5	1
3	7	2	5	8	1	4	9	6
7	8	9	4	2	3	1	6	5
4	6	3	8	1	5	9	7	2
1	2	5	7	9	6	8	4	3
6	3	8	2	4	9	5	1	7
2	4	1	3	5	7	6	8	9
9	5	7	1	6	8	2	3	4

Solutions 85–96

85

7	9	6	5	8	1	4	3	2
4	1	3	2	6	7	5	9	8
8	2	5	3	4	9	1	6	7
6	7	4	8	1	5	3	2	9
3	8	1	6	9	2	7	4	5
9	5	2	4	7	3	6	8	1
1	3	8	7	2	4	9	5	6
2	4	9	1	5	6	8	7	3
5	6	7	9	3	8	2	1	4

86

8	9	6	1	3	5	2	7	4
7	4	2	8	6	9	3	5	1
3	1	5	2	7	4	6	8	9
2	5	7	9	8	6	4	1	3
9	8	4	5	1	3	7	2	6
6	3	1	4	2	7	8	9	5
1	7	3	6	9	2	5	4	8
5	6	8	7	4	1	9	3	2
4	2	9	3	5	8	1	6	7

87

4	7	2	3	1	9	6	5	8
1	6	8	4	5	7	2	9	3
5	9	3	6	8	2	4	1	7
6	5	1	7	9	8	3	2	4
8	3	7	2	4	5	9	6	1
2	4	9	1	6	3	8	7	5
9	1	4	5	3	6	7	8	2
3	2	6	8	7	1	5	4	9
7	8	5	9	2	4	1	3	6

88

6	5	7	9	4	1	3	2	8
1	8	4	7	3	2	5	6	9
2	9	3	6	8	5	7	4	1
8	3	1	4	2	7	9	5	6
9	4	5	8	6	3	1	7	2
7	6	2	5	1	9	8	3	4
3	2	9	1	7	6	4	8	5
5	7	8	2	9	4	6	1	3
4	1	6	3	5	8	2	9	7

89

6	2	9	5	8	3	7	1	4
7	8	3	6	4	1	5	2	9
1	5	4	2	9	7	3	8	6
8	3	7	1	2	4	6	9	5
4	1	6	9	5	8	2	7	3
2	9	5	3	7	6	8	4	1
3	4	2	7	1	5	9	6	8
5	7	1	8	6	9	4	3	2
9	6	8	4	3	2	1	5	7

90

4	9	6	3	1	8	7	2	5
5	7	3	4	2	6	8	1	9
8	1	2	9	7	5	4	6	3
7	3	1	6	5	2	9	4	8
9	2	8	7	4	3	1	5	6
6	5	4	8	9	1	2	3	7
3	4	7	1	6	9	5	8	2
1	8	5	2	3	7	6	9	4
2	6	9	5	8	4	3	7	1

91

1	8	7	4	3	2	6	5	9
5	2	9	6	8	7	3	4	1
4	6	3	9	5	1	2	8	7
9	1	8	2	4	6	7	3	5
2	7	6	5	1	3	8	9	4
3	4	5	7	9	8	1	2	6
8	9	2	1	7	4	5	6	3
7	3	4	8	6	5	9	1	2
6	5	1	3	2	9	4	7	8

92

5	7	3	4	1	9	6	8	2
6	2	8	5	3	7	9	4	1
9	4	1	2	6	8	7	3	5
3	1	6	7	8	2	5	9	4
4	8	9	1	5	3	2	7	6
2	5	7	9	4	6	3	1	8
8	3	4	6	9	5	1	2	7
7	9	5	8	2	1	4	6	3
1	6	2	3	7	4	8	5	9

93

5	7	4	8	9	1	2	3	6
2	3	8	7	6	5	1	9	4
9	1	6	2	4	3	5	7	8
6	9	1	4	2	8	7	5	3
4	5	7	1	3	6	8	2	9
3	8	2	5	7	9	6	4	1
1	4	5	3	8	7	9	6	2
7	6	3	9	1	2	4	8	5
8	2	9	6	5	4	3	1	7

94

9	5	6	7	3	1	4	2	8
8	3	1	6	4	2	9	7	5
7	4	2	9	5	8	3	6	1
5	8	4	1	9	6	7	3	2
6	2	3	4	8	7	1	5	9
1	7	9	5	2	3	6	8	4
3	9	8	2	6	4	5	1	7
4	6	7	8	1	5	2	9	3
2	1	5	3	7	9	8	4	6

95

1	3	2	8	6	4	7	5	9
7	9	6	3	1	5	2	4	8
5	8	4	7	9	2	1	6	3
2	7	1	5	8	9	4	3	6
4	5	3	6	7	1	9	8	2
8	6	9	4	2	3	5	7	1
9	4	5	1	3	6	8	2	7
6	1	7	2	5	8	3	9	4
3	2	8	9	4	7	6	1	5

96

9	2	5	7	6	8	1	3	4
7	6	3	1	5	4	9	2	8
4	8	1	2	9	3	5	6	7
8	5	4	9	1	6	2	7	3
2	3	7	8	4	5	6	9	1
6	1	9	3	7	2	8	4	5
1	9	6	4	8	7	3	5	2
3	7	8	5	2	9	4	1	6
5	4	2	6	3	1	7	8	9

Solutions 97–108

97

8	7	5	6	3	1	9	4	2
6	3	1	9	2	4	7	8	5
9	4	2	5	7	8	3	6	1
5	8	6	3	4	9	1	2	7
3	9	7	2	1	6	8	5	4
1	2	4	7	8	5	6	3	9
7	1	3	4	6	2	5	9	8
2	5	8	1	9	3	4	7	6
4	6	9	8	5	7	2	1	3

98

9	6	2	7	3	1	8	5	4
5	1	4	9	8	6	7	2	3
3	7	8	4	5	2	6	9	1
2	8	6	3	4	9	5	1	7
1	9	3	2	7	5	4	6	8
4	5	7	6	1	8	2	3	9
8	3	5	1	2	4	9	7	6
6	4	1	5	9	7	3	8	2
7	2	9	8	6	3	1	4	5

99

8	9	7	2	3	5	6	1	4
4	1	5	7	8	6	9	3	2
6	3	2	4	1	9	7	8	5
3	6	9	5	7	2	1	4	8
2	7	4	1	6	8	5	9	3
1	5	8	3	9	4	2	6	7
5	8	3	9	2	1	4	7	6
9	4	6	8	5	7	3	2	1
7	2	1	6	4	3	8	5	9

100

9	3	1	8	5	4	2	6	7
8	5	2	1	6	7	9	4	3
4	7	6	2	9	3	5	8	1
5	4	9	7	2	1	6	3	8
3	6	7	9	4	8	1	5	2
2	1	8	6	3	5	4	7	9
6	9	3	5	7	2	8	1	4
7	8	5	4	1	9	3	2	6
1	2	4	3	8	6	7	9	5

101

9	4	1	6	5	2	3	8	7
5	8	2	7	3	1	6	9	4
7	3	6	4	9	8	2	1	5
3	1	9	2	4	7	8	5	6
8	2	5	9	1	6	4	7	3
6	7	4	3	8	5	1	2	9
4	6	7	8	2	9	5	3	1
1	9	8	5	6	3	7	4	2
2	5	3	1	7	4	9	6	8

102

3	4	2	5	7	6	1	9	8
9	1	6	3	8	2	4	7	5
7	8	5	4	1	9	3	2	6
1	3	8	2	5	7	9	6	4
6	5	4	1	9	3	7	8	2
2	7	9	8	6	4	5	1	3
4	2	7	9	3	8	6	5	1
8	9	1	6	4	5	2	3	7
5	6	3	7	2	1	8	4	9

103

4	6	8	9	3	2	7	1	5
7	5	9	1	6	4	3	8	2
3	2	1	8	7	5	4	6	9
6	7	2	5	9	8	1	4	3
1	4	5	3	2	7	6	9	8
8	9	3	4	1	6	2	5	7
5	8	7	6	4	3	9	2	1
9	3	6	2	5	1	8	7	4
2	1	4	7	8	9	5	3	6

104

4	5	2	6	8	7	3	1	9
1	6	9	4	3	5	7	2	8
8	7	3	2	9	1	4	6	5
6	4	5	8	2	3	9	7	1
3	2	1	9	7	6	5	8	4
7	9	8	5	1	4	2	3	6
2	8	6	3	4	9	1	5	7
9	3	7	1	5	8	6	4	2
5	1	4	7	6	2	8	9	3

105

4	8	2	3	7	6	1	5	9
9	1	5	4	8	2	7	3	6
6	3	7	9	1	5	4	2	8
7	5	6	2	3	1	9	8	4
2	9	1	5	4	8	3	6	7
3	4	8	7	6	9	5	1	2
8	2	9	1	5	4	6	7	3
1	6	3	8	9	7	2	4	5
5	7	4	6	2	3	8	9	1

106

3	2	9	8	4	7	1	5	6
4	1	8	6	2	5	3	7	9
6	5	7	9	1	3	4	8	2
2	9	6	5	3	4	7	1	8
1	8	5	7	6	9	2	3	4
7	4	3	1	8	2	6	9	5
9	6	2	3	7	8	5	4	1
8	3	4	2	5	1	9	6	7
5	7	1	4	9	6	8	2	3

107

4	1	9	7	5	3	6	8	2
8	6	2	9	1	4	5	3	7
3	5	7	2	6	8	1	9	4
9	8	1	4	7	2	3	5	6
7	3	4	6	9	5	2	1	8
5	2	6	8	3	1	4	7	9
6	9	3	5	2	7	8	4	1
2	4	5	1	8	9	7	6	3
1	7	8	3	4	6	9	2	5

108

9	6	2	7	8	5	3	4	1
5	4	3	1	6	9	8	7	2
1	8	7	2	4	3	6	5	9
7	9	8	5	1	2	4	6	3
6	1	5	4	3	7	9	2	8
2	3	4	8	9	6	5	1	7
3	5	9	6	7	1	2	8	4
8	7	6	9	2	4	1	3	5
4	2	1	3	5	8	7	9	6

Solutions 109–120

109

1	4	3	5	9	2	6	8	7
5	9	8	1	6	7	2	3	4
2	6	7	8	4	3	1	9	5
6	7	1	3	8	5	9	4	2
4	2	9	6	7	1	3	5	8
3	8	5	4	2	9	7	1	6
7	5	6	9	1	4	8	2	3
9	3	2	7	5	8	4	6	1
8	1	4	2	3	6	5	7	9

110

7	1	2	8	9	6	5	4	3
9	4	3	5	7	2	8	6	1
5	6	8	3	4	1	7	2	9
8	2	6	4	5	9	1	3	7
1	5	9	7	6	3	4	8	2
3	7	4	2	1	8	9	5	6
2	8	7	1	3	4	6	9	5
4	9	5	6	2	7	3	1	8
6	3	1	9	8	5	2	7	4

111

6	3	4	7	1	5	9	8	2
1	9	2	8	3	4	6	7	5
5	7	8	9	2	6	3	1	4
8	1	7	3	6	2	5	4	9
9	5	3	1	4	7	8	2	6
2	4	6	5	8	9	1	3	7
3	6	5	4	7	1	2	9	8
7	8	9	2	5	3	4	6	1
4	2	1	6	9	8	7	5	3

112

5	3	7	8	9	6	2	1	4
2	8	9	4	1	5	6	7	3
6	1	4	7	2	3	9	5	8
8	7	5	1	4	9	3	6	2
9	4	1	3	6	2	5	8	7
3	6	2	5	8	7	1	4	9
1	9	3	6	7	4	8	2	5
4	2	8	9	5	1	7	3	6
7	5	6	2	3	8	4	9	1

113

5	2	1	9	8	4	7	6	3
7	4	3	6	5	1	9	8	2
8	6	9	3	7	2	4	5	1
9	8	4	1	6	5	2	3	7
6	1	7	2	3	8	5	9	4
3	5	2	4	9	7	8	1	6
1	9	5	7	2	3	6	4	8
2	3	6	8	4	9	1	7	5
4	7	8	5	1	6	3	2	9

114

2	9	8	5	4	6	3	1	7
6	5	3	2	7	1	9	4	8
4	1	7	8	9	3	5	2	6
7	6	9	1	3	5	4	8	2
3	8	4	6	2	9	7	5	1
1	2	5	7	8	4	6	9	3
9	7	1	3	5	2	8	6	4
5	3	2	4	6	8	1	7	9
8	4	6	9	1	7	2	3	5

115

1	7	4	8	9	6	5	2	3
3	2	6	4	7	5	1	9	8
9	8	5	3	2	1	4	6	7
7	4	9	1	8	3	6	5	2
8	6	3	2	5	4	9	7	1
5	1	2	9	6	7	8	3	4
4	9	7	6	3	8	2	1	5
6	3	8	5	1	2	7	4	9
2	5	1	7	4	9	3	8	6

116

9	4	2	8	1	5	3	6	7
1	7	5	3	2	6	8	9	4
3	8	6	7	9	4	5	2	1
4	6	3	9	8	1	2	7	5
8	1	7	5	3	2	9	4	6
5	2	9	4	6	7	1	8	3
6	5	1	2	4	8	7	3	9
7	3	8	6	5	9	4	1	2
2	9	4	1	7	3	6	5	8

117

8	2	5	6	1	4	9	7	3
9	4	6	7	2	3	1	8	5
3	1	7	8	5	9	2	4	6
6	5	9	4	7	2	8	3	1
4	3	8	1	9	6	5	2	7
2	7	1	5	3	8	4	6	9
5	6	3	2	8	1	7	9	4
1	8	4	9	6	7	3	5	2
7	9	2	3	4	5	6	1	8

118

9	8	7	4	1	6	5	3	2
5	6	3	8	2	7	4	9	1
4	1	2	5	3	9	8	7	6
8	3	5	9	4	2	6	1	7
6	2	9	1	7	5	3	4	8
1	7	4	3	6	8	2	5	9
3	9	6	2	5	1	7	8	4
7	5	8	6	9	4	1	2	3
2	4	1	7	8	3	9	6	5

119

1	5	4	2	6	9	8	7	3
7	3	2	4	5	8	6	1	9
6	8	9	3	7	1	2	4	5
2	4	6	8	1	3	9	5	7
8	9	3	5	2	7	4	6	1
5	7	1	9	4	6	3	2	8
9	1	7	6	3	2	5	8	4
3	6	5	7	8	4	1	9	2
4	2	8	1	9	5	7	3	6

120

6	8	5	1	3	2	9	4	7
7	4	9	8	5	6	3	1	2
1	2	3	9	7	4	6	5	8
5	7	6	4	8	3	1	2	9
3	1	8	2	6	9	5	7	4
2	9	4	7	1	5	8	6	3
4	3	1	5	9	7	2	8	6
8	6	7	3	2	1	4	9	5
9	5	2	6	4	8	7	3	1

Solutions 121–132

121

8	2	3	9	1	4	7	5	6
1	6	4	5	7	3	8	9	2
5	9	7	8	6	2	4	3	1
9	7	2	3	4	8	6	1	5
4	5	8	1	2	6	9	7	3
3	1	6	7	9	5	2	4	8
6	4	5	2	3	7	1	8	9
2	8	1	4	5	9	3	6	7
7	3	9	6	8	1	5	2	4

122

3	2	1	6	8	4	5	7	9
7	8	4	5	9	3	2	6	1
5	9	6	7	2	1	4	3	8
2	4	5	8	7	9	6	1	3
9	1	7	3	6	2	8	5	4
6	3	8	4	1	5	9	2	7
4	6	3	1	5	8	7	9	2
1	7	2	9	4	6	3	8	5
8	5	9	2	3	7	1	4	6

123

7	1	9	8	2	6	5	3	4
2	3	5	7	4	1	6	8	9
4	8	6	9	3	5	7	2	1
1	6	4	5	8	2	9	7	3
9	7	8	4	1	3	2	5	6
5	2	3	6	9	7	1	4	8
6	4	2	3	5	9	8	1	7
8	9	1	2	7	4	3	6	5
3	5	7	1	6	8	4	9	2

124

9	1	2	3	7	5	4	8	6
8	7	6	4	2	9	5	1	3
3	4	5	6	1	8	9	7	2
1	6	9	7	3	4	2	5	8
7	8	3	9	5	2	6	4	1
5	2	4	8	6	1	7	3	9
2	3	8	5	4	6	1	9	7
6	5	7	1	9	3	8	2	4
4	9	1	2	8	7	3	6	5

125

7	8	2	1	3	4	5	9	6
4	9	1	6	5	2	3	8	7
6	5	3	9	8	7	2	4	1
1	3	8	5	7	9	6	2	4
9	2	6	3	4	1	7	5	8
5	7	4	2	6	8	9	1	3
2	6	9	8	1	3	4	7	5
3	1	7	4	2	5	8	6	9
8	4	5	7	9	6	1	3	2

126

4	3	1	9	5	7	6	8	2
2	6	7	8	4	1	5	9	3
8	9	5	6	2	3	1	4	7
5	4	9	3	7	6	2	1	8
3	2	6	1	8	5	4	7	9
7	1	8	4	9	2	3	6	5
6	7	3	5	1	8	9	2	4
9	5	2	7	6	4	8	3	1
1	8	4	2	3	9	7	5	6

127

3	9	1	4	5	8	7	6	2
6	4	8	2	1	7	9	5	3
7	5	2	9	6	3	4	8	1
9	2	5	8	4	1	6	3	7
4	6	3	5	7	9	1	2	8
1	8	7	3	2	6	5	4	9
2	7	9	6	8	5	3	1	4
8	1	6	7	3	4	2	9	5
5	3	4	1	9	2	8	7	6

128

2	6	4	7	3	5	8	1	9
5	9	1	4	8	6	3	2	7
8	3	7	9	1	2	6	5	4
9	2	8	1	4	7	5	6	3
7	4	3	6	5	8	1	9	2
1	5	6	3	2	9	7	4	8
3	1	5	2	7	4	9	8	6
4	8	9	5	6	3	2	7	1
6	7	2	8	9	1	4	3	5

129

3	5	6	4	7	2	9	1	8
4	2	9	5	8	1	3	6	7
8	1	7	9	6	3	5	4	2
2	4	3	6	1	7	8	5	9
1	7	5	2	9	8	4	3	6
9	6	8	3	5	4	2	7	1
5	3	1	8	2	6	7	9	4
6	9	2	7	4	5	1	8	3
7	8	4	1	3	9	6	2	5

130

3	9	6	7	1	5	4	8	2
8	2	4	9	6	3	1	7	5
7	1	5	2	8	4	6	9	3
9	7	3	1	4	2	8	5	6
1	4	8	5	7	6	2	3	9
6	5	2	8	3	9	7	4	1
2	3	7	6	5	8	9	1	4
5	8	9	4	2	1	3	6	7
4	6	1	3	9	7	5	2	8

131

4	5	9	6	7	1	2	3	8
3	2	7	9	5	8	4	1	6
6	1	8	2	3	4	9	5	7
7	6	4	5	9	2	3	8	1
9	3	1	8	4	7	5	6	2
5	8	2	1	6	3	7	4	9
2	7	6	4	1	5	8	9	3
1	4	3	7	8	9	6	2	5
8	9	5	3	2	6	1	7	4

132

6	9	8	3	4	5	1	7	2
1	4	3	2	6	7	9	5	8
7	5	2	9	8	1	3	6	4
5	7	9	6	1	4	2	8	3
4	2	1	8	5	3	7	9	6
8	3	6	7	2	9	5	4	1
9	8	7	4	3	2	6	1	5
2	1	4	5	7	6	8	3	9
3	6	5	1	9	8	4	2	7

Solutions 133–144

133

9	8	6	3	2	4	5	1	7
2	4	5	7	9	1	8	3	6
1	7	3	8	6	5	4	9	2
8	5	7	2	1	3	6	4	9
6	9	1	5	4	7	3	2	8
4	3	2	9	8	6	7	5	1
3	2	8	6	5	9	1	7	4
7	6	4	1	3	2	9	8	5
5	1	9	4	7	8	2	6	3

134

1	9	7	8	2	3	5	6	4
8	4	3	5	6	7	9	2	1
2	5	6	9	1	4	7	3	8
5	3	9	6	8	1	4	7	2
7	8	2	3	4	5	1	9	6
6	1	4	7	9	2	8	5	3
3	2	5	1	7	8	6	4	9
4	6	8	2	5	9	3	1	7
9	7	1	4	3	6	2	8	5

135

5	4	1	2	3	8	7	9	6
3	8	7	6	4	9	2	5	1
6	9	2	1	7	5	8	4	3
2	3	6	5	9	7	1	8	4
1	5	8	3	2	4	6	7	9
4	7	9	8	1	6	3	2	5
9	1	4	7	8	3	5	6	2
7	6	3	9	5	2	4	1	8
8	2	5	4	6	1	9	3	7

136

6	3	2	8	7	5	1	4	9
5	7	9	1	3	4	2	6	8
4	8	1	2	6	9	5	7	3
1	2	5	9	8	7	6	3	4
3	6	8	5	4	1	9	2	7
7	9	4	6	2	3	8	1	5
2	4	6	3	9	8	7	5	1
8	1	7	4	5	2	3	9	6
9	5	3	7	1	6	4	8	2

137

6	9	3	7	8	2	1	5	4
5	8	4	6	9	1	2	3	7
7	1	2	3	5	4	8	6	9
8	7	9	4	3	6	5	2	1
3	4	5	2	1	8	9	7	6
1	2	6	5	7	9	4	8	3
2	6	8	9	4	7	3	1	5
9	3	1	8	6	5	7	4	2
4	5	7	1	2	3	6	9	8

138

5	6	7	8	3	1	4	2	9
1	2	8	9	4	6	3	7	5
3	4	9	2	5	7	8	1	6
8	7	2	1	6	5	9	3	4
9	1	4	3	8	2	6	5	7
6	5	3	4	7	9	2	8	1
2	8	1	5	9	4	7	6	3
4	3	6	7	1	8	5	9	2
7	9	5	6	2	3	1	4	8

139

5	4	7	8	9	2	1	3	6
9	8	3	6	4	1	2	5	7
2	6	1	7	3	5	8	9	4
4	1	6	5	2	3	7	8	9
7	9	2	4	1	8	5	6	3
3	5	8	9	7	6	4	1	2
8	7	9	1	6	4	3	2	5
1	2	4	3	5	9	6	7	8
6	3	5	2	8	7	9	4	1

140

6	4	8	5	9	7	3	1	2
7	3	2	8	1	4	9	5	6
9	1	5	3	2	6	8	7	4
4	6	3	1	5	9	7	2	8
8	5	1	7	6	2	4	3	9
2	7	9	4	3	8	1	6	5
3	9	4	6	7	5	2	8	1
5	8	7	2	4	1	6	9	3
1	2	6	9	8	3	5	4	7

141

4	2	5	7	1	8	3	6	9
6	8	3	2	5	9	4	1	7
7	9	1	3	4	6	2	5	8
5	6	4	8	9	2	7	3	1
2	3	8	5	7	1	6	9	4
9	1	7	6	3	4	8	2	5
3	5	2	1	8	7	9	4	6
1	7	9	4	6	3	5	8	2
8	4	6	9	2	5	1	7	3

142

9	7	4	6	3	1	5	8	2
6	2	1	7	8	5	4	3	9
8	5	3	9	2	4	6	1	7
5	1	8	3	6	2	7	9	4
2	4	7	1	9	8	3	6	5
3	9	6	4	5	7	8	2	1
1	8	5	2	4	6	9	7	3
4	3	2	8	7	9	1	5	6
7	6	9	5	1	3	2	4	8

143

5	1	9	7	2	4	8	6	3
3	6	8	9	5	1	7	2	4
2	4	7	3	8	6	5	1	9
4	5	6	1	3	8	2	9	7
1	8	3	2	9	7	6	4	5
9	7	2	6	4	5	1	3	8
7	9	4	8	6	2	3	5	1
8	2	5	4	1	3	9	7	6
6	3	1	5	7	9	4	8	2

144

2	5	1	8	6	9	4	3	7
6	7	9	4	3	1	2	8	5
3	8	4	5	7	2	9	6	1
8	9	6	3	1	4	7	5	2
5	4	7	2	8	6	3	1	9
1	3	2	9	5	7	6	4	8
7	6	5	1	2	3	8	9	4
9	1	3	7	4	8	5	2	6
4	2	8	6	9	5	1	7	3

Solutions 145–156

145

8	2	3	1	7	9	5	6	4
5	6	9	2	8	4	3	7	1
7	1	4	3	5	6	9	2	8
4	3	6	9	2	8	7	1	5
2	9	5	6	1	7	8	4	3
1	8	7	4	3	5	2	9	6
3	4	2	8	9	1	6	5	7
9	7	1	5	6	3	4	8	2
6	5	8	7	4	2	1	3	9

146

8	1	4	7	3	9	2	5	6
2	7	3	6	5	1	4	9	8
5	6	9	2	4	8	7	1	3
6	9	2	8	1	4	5	3	7
4	8	7	3	6	5	9	2	1
1	3	5	9	7	2	6	8	4
9	2	1	4	8	6	3	7	5
7	5	6	1	9	3	8	4	2
3	4	8	5	2	7	1	6	9

147

3	4	6	7	2	9	8	5	1
5	9	1	4	3	8	2	6	7
2	7	8	1	5	6	4	9	3
7	1	9	5	6	4	3	2	8
4	6	3	2	8	7	9	1	5
8	5	2	3	9	1	7	4	6
6	8	5	9	4	3	1	7	2
9	2	7	8	1	5	6	3	4
1	3	4	6	7	2	5	8	9

148

7	5	8	6	2	1	4	9	3
3	9	2	7	5	4	8	6	1
1	4	6	9	3	8	2	5	7
6	3	9	1	7	2	5	8	4
8	1	5	3	4	6	7	2	9
2	7	4	8	9	5	1	3	6
4	6	7	5	8	3	9	1	2
9	8	1	2	6	7	3	4	5
5	2	3	4	1	9	6	7	8

149

9	5	2	8	1	6	3	4	7
4	1	8	3	7	9	5	2	6
7	3	6	2	4	5	1	8	9
5	8	3	4	6	1	9	7	2
6	9	4	7	3	2	8	1	5
1	2	7	9	5	8	6	3	4
8	6	9	1	2	7	4	5	3
3	7	1	5	9	4	2	6	8
2	4	5	6	8	3	7	9	1

150

7	1	6	9	4	2	5	3	8
2	8	9	6	5	3	1	4	7
5	3	4	1	7	8	2	9	6
9	2	3	4	1	6	7	8	5
1	6	5	3	8	7	9	2	4
8	4	7	2	9	5	6	1	3
3	7	1	5	2	4	8	6	9
6	9	8	7	3	1	4	5	2
4	5	2	8	6	9	3	7	1

151

9	8	4	1	2	3	7	5	6
3	2	7	5	6	9	4	1	8
5	6	1	4	7	8	2	3	9
2	3	9	6	1	7	5	8	4
1	7	5	8	3	4	9	6	2
6	4	8	2	9	5	1	7	3
7	1	2	3	4	6	8	9	5
4	5	6	9	8	1	3	2	7
8	9	3	7	5	2	6	4	1

152

4	3	1	8	9	5	2	6	7
8	5	2	6	1	7	4	3	9
7	9	6	2	3	4	5	1	8
1	6	7	9	2	3	8	4	5
3	2	9	4	5	8	6	7	1
5	8	4	1	7	6	9	2	3
9	7	5	3	6	2	1	8	4
6	1	8	7	4	9	3	5	2
2	4	3	5	8	1	7	9	6

153

3	9	4	5	6	2	7	8	1
2	5	7	4	8	1	9	6	3
6	8	1	3	9	7	4	2	5
1	3	6	2	7	5	8	9	4
4	2	9	8	1	3	5	7	6
8	7	5	9	4	6	3	1	2
9	6	2	7	5	4	1	3	8
5	1	8	6	3	9	2	4	7
7	4	3	1	2	8	6	5	9

154

1	5	6	4	9	8	7	3	2
3	9	4	7	5	2	6	1	8
7	2	8	3	6	1	4	9	5
5	6	9	2	3	4	8	7	1
2	3	7	1	8	9	5	6	4
8	4	1	6	7	5	9	2	3
9	1	3	8	4	6	2	5	7
6	8	2	5	1	7	3	4	9
4	7	5	9	2	3	1	8	6

155

1	8	4	5	3	2	6	9	7
7	6	9	1	4	8	3	5	2
5	2	3	7	6	9	4	8	1
9	3	7	6	8	4	2	1	5
4	5	8	2	7	1	9	3	6
2	1	6	3	9	5	8	7	4
6	9	1	8	2	7	5	4	3
3	4	5	9	1	6	7	2	8
8	7	2	4	5	3	1	6	9

156

8	6	7	5	3	2	4	1	9
4	9	2	8	7	1	3	6	5
5	3	1	9	4	6	8	7	2
1	5	8	3	6	9	7	2	4
9	4	6	7	2	8	1	5	3
7	2	3	4	1	5	9	8	6
2	1	4	6	8	3	5	9	7
3	8	9	2	5	7	6	4	1
6	7	5	1	9	4	2	3	8

Solutions 181–192

181

8	6	5	9	3	4	2	1	7
7	4	3	1	8	2	6	9	5
9	2	1	6	5	7	4	3	8
6	3	7	2	1	9	8	5	4
1	8	4	7	6	5	9	2	3
2	5	9	3	4	8	1	7	6
5	9	2	4	7	6	3	8	1
3	7	6	8	9	1	5	4	2
4	1	8	5	2	3	7	6	9

182

8	4	6	1	7	5	3	9	2
9	7	5	4	3	2	1	8	6
3	1	2	6	9	8	4	5	7
6	2	3	8	5	7	9	4	1
4	5	8	9	2	1	7	6	3
7	9	1	3	6	4	8	2	5
1	6	9	5	4	3	2	7	8
5	8	7	2	1	9	6	3	4
2	3	4	7	8	6	5	1	9

183

3	2	8	6	9	1	4	5	7
4	9	6	5	3	7	8	1	2
5	7	1	2	8	4	6	9	3
2	1	9	7	6	5	3	8	4
7	4	5	3	1	8	9	2	6
8	6	3	4	2	9	1	7	5
6	8	2	9	5	3	7	4	1
9	3	7	1	4	2	5	6	8
1	5	4	8	7	6	2	3	9

184

8	3	4	9	5	6	7	1	2
5	7	1	2	3	4	6	8	9
6	2	9	8	7	1	4	5	3
7	9	3	5	4	8	2	6	1
2	5	8	6	1	3	9	4	7
1	4	6	7	2	9	8	3	5
4	6	7	3	9	5	1	2	8
9	8	5	1	6	2	3	7	4
3	1	2	4	8	7	5	9	6

185

1	6	3	4	2	9	7	5	8
4	7	8	5	1	3	2	9	6
5	9	2	8	6	7	1	4	3
6	3	7	9	5	2	4	8	1
8	1	9	6	3	4	5	7	2
2	5	4	7	8	1	6	3	9
3	8	5	1	7	6	9	2	4
9	2	1	3	4	5	8	6	7
7	4	6	2	9	8	3	1	5

186

7	1	3	8	6	9	4	5	2
8	6	5	4	2	3	7	1	9
4	2	9	5	1	7	6	3	8
3	9	6	2	7	8	1	4	5
2	5	7	3	4	1	8	9	6
1	4	8	6	9	5	3	2	7
5	7	2	1	3	6	9	8	4
9	3	4	7	8	2	5	6	1
6	8	1	9	5	4	2	7	3

187

2	7	8	4	5	9	3	1	6
5	9	6	3	8	1	7	2	4
3	4	1	7	2	6	8	5	9
1	2	7	5	4	3	9	6	8
6	5	3	1	9	8	2	4	7
4	8	9	6	7	2	1	3	5
8	3	4	9	1	5	6	7	2
7	1	2	8	6	4	5	9	3
9	6	5	2	3	7	4	8	1

188

5	1	3	2	8	7	4	6	9
7	6	4	9	5	3	1	2	8
8	2	9	6	4	1	3	5	7
4	5	6	3	9	8	2	7	1
3	7	2	1	6	5	8	9	4
9	8	1	4	7	2	5	3	6
1	9	5	7	3	4	6	8	2
2	3	7	8	1	6	9	4	5
6	4	8	5	2	9	7	1	3

189

2	6	1	3	7	5	4	8	9
7	9	3	8	4	2	6	1	5
4	5	8	9	6	1	3	2	7
9	8	5	2	1	6	7	3	4
1	7	2	4	5	3	8	9	6
3	4	6	7	9	8	2	5	1
8	1	4	6	3	9	5	7	2
6	2	9	5	8	7	1	4	3
5	3	7	1	2	4	9	6	8

190

4	7	5	6	9	2	8	1	3
3	2	9	4	1	8	5	6	7
8	6	1	3	7	5	2	4	9
2	4	3	1	6	9	7	5	8
1	5	8	7	2	3	6	9	4
7	9	6	5	8	4	1	3	2
9	8	4	2	5	1	3	7	6
6	1	2	9	3	7	4	8	5
5	3	7	8	4	6	9	2	1

191

5	4	8	2	9	6	3	1	7
2	7	1	3	8	5	6	9	4
3	6	9	1	7	4	2	5	8
6	2	7	9	3	1	4	8	5
4	1	3	8	5	2	7	6	9
8	9	5	6	4	7	1	3	2
7	3	4	5	1	8	9	2	6
9	5	6	7	2	3	8	4	1
1	8	2	4	6	9	5	7	3

192

3	7	5	2	9	6	8	4	1
9	2	1	4	3	8	7	5	6
6	8	4	7	5	1	2	9	3
4	9	2	5	7	3	6	1	8
1	5	3	8	6	2	9	7	4
8	6	7	1	4	9	5	3	2
7	1	6	9	2	4	3	8	5
2	4	9	3	8	5	1	6	7
5	3	8	6	1	7	4	2	9

Solutions 193–201

193

7	3	9	2	5	8	4	6	1
6	4	5	7	1	3	9	8	2
8	1	2	9	4	6	3	7	5
1	9	6	8	3	2	5	4	7
5	7	4	1	6	9	2	3	8
3	2	8	5	7	4	1	9	6
9	5	7	3	8	1	6	2	4
4	8	3	6	2	5	7	1	9
2	6	1	4	9	7	8	5	3

194

7	8	2	4	3	9	1	6	5
6	4	9	5	7	1	3	2	8
1	3	5	8	6	2	9	7	4
4	6	7	3	9	8	2	5	1
9	5	1	2	4	7	8	3	6
8	2	3	1	5	6	7	4	9
5	1	4	9	2	3	6	8	7
3	7	8	6	1	5	4	9	2
2	9	6	7	8	4	5	1	3

195

4	9	6	5	8	3	1	2	7
5	8	1	4	7	2	9	6	3
3	7	2	9	1	6	8	5	4
2	4	8	7	9	5	3	1	6
1	3	5	6	2	4	7	8	9
9	6	7	1	3	8	5	4	2
8	1	4	3	6	9	2	7	5
7	5	9	2	4	1	6	3	8
6	2	3	8	5	7	4	9	1

196

5	9	6	1	3	7	4	8	2
1	8	4	6	9	2	3	7	5
2	7	3	4	8	5	1	9	6
6	2	8	3	4	9	7	5	1
7	4	5	2	1	8	9	6	3
3	1	9	5	7	6	8	2	4
4	5	7	9	6	1	2	3	8
8	6	1	7	2	3	5	4	9
9	3	2	8	5	4	6	1	7

197

7	5	6	2	1	3	8	4	9
8	1	3	4	5	9	7	6	2
4	9	2	7	8	6	3	5	1
3	4	1	6	9	2	5	7	8
2	6	9	5	7	8	1	3	4
5	7	8	3	4	1	9	2	6
6	8	5	9	2	7	4	1	3
9	3	4	1	6	5	2	8	7
1	2	7	8	3	4	6	9	5

198

1	9	3	5	8	4	7	6	2
7	5	2	9	3	6	4	1	8
8	4	6	2	7	1	5	9	3
4	7	8	6	9	3	2	5	1
2	6	5	4	1	7	3	8	9
3	1	9	8	2	5	6	7	4
6	2	1	3	5	9	8	4	7
5	3	7	1	4	8	9	2	6
9	8	4	7	6	2	1	3	5

199

9	1	2	6	7	5	3	4	8
3	4	8	2	9	1	6	5	7
5	7	6	3	4	8	1	2	9
2	9	7	1	5	4	8	3	6
6	5	4	7	8	3	9	1	2
1	8	3	9	2	6	4	7	5
4	2	1	5	6	9	7	8	3
7	3	9	8	1	2	5	6	4
8	6	5	4	3	7	2	9	1

200

5	4	9	8	6	7	3	2	1
3	2	6	1	4	9	7	8	5
1	8	7	5	2	3	9	4	6
6	9	8	2	7	4	5	1	3
2	3	5	6	8	1	4	9	7
7	1	4	9	3	5	2	6	8
8	5	1	7	9	2	6	3	4
9	6	3	4	5	8	1	7	2
4	7	2	3	1	6	8	5	9

201

1	7	9	4	3	6	8	5	2
2	4	8	1	5	9	6	7	3
3	6	5	7	8	2	4	1	9
9	1	3	8	4	5	2	6	7
5	2	4	6	9	7	1	3	8
6	8	7	2	1	3	9	4	5
7	9	1	5	2	4	3	8	6
8	3	6	9	7	1	5	2	4
4	5	2	3	6	8	7	9	1